NATIONS OF THE MODERN WORLD

CEYLON | S. A. Pakeman
Formerly Professor of Modern History, Ceylon University College; Appointed Member, House of Representatives, Ceylon, 1947–52

MODERN EGYPT | Tom Little
Managing Director and General Manager of Regional News Services (Middle East), Ltd., London

ENGLAND
A Portrait | John Bowle
Professor of Political Theory, Collège d'Europe, Bruges

MODERN INDIA | Sir Percival Griffiths
President of the India, Pakistan and Burma Association

MODERN IRAN | Peter Avery
Lecturer in Persian and Fellow of King's College, Cambridge

JAPAN | Sir Esler Dening
H.M. Ambassador to Japan, 1952–57

MALAYA | J. M. Gullick
Formerly of the Malayan Civil Service

MOROCCO | Mark I. Cohen
and
Lorna Hahn

NIGERIA | Sir Rex Niven
Colonial Service, Nigeria, 1921–59; Member of Northern House of Assembly, 1947–59

NEW ZEALAND | James W. Rowe
Director of New Zealand Institute of Economic Research, Inc.
Margaret A. Rowe
Tutor in English, Victoria University, Wellington

PAKISTAN	Ian Stephens *Formerly Editor of* The Statesman *Calcutta and Delhi, 1942–51; Fellow of King's College, Cambridge, 1952–58*
SOUTH AFRICA	John Cope *Formerly Editor-in-Chief of* The Forum; *South African Correspondent of* The Guardian
SUDAN REPUBLIC	K. D. D. Henderson *Formerly of the Sudan Political Service; Governor of Darfur Province, 1949–53*
TURKEY	Geoffrey Lewis *Senior Lecturer in Islamic Studies, Oxford*
THE UNITED STATES OF AMERICA	H. C. Allen *Commonwealth Fund Professor of American History, University College, London*
YUGOSLAVIA	Muriel Heppell and F. B. Singleton

NEW ZEALAND

NEW ZEALAND

By

JAMES W. ROWE

and

MARGARET A. ROWE

FREDERICK A. PRAEGER, *Publishers*

New York · Washington

BOOKS THAT MATTER

Published in the United States of America in 1968
by Frederick A. Praeger, Inc., Publishers
111 Fourth Avenue, New York, N.Y. 10003

© 1967 in London, England, by James W. Rowe and
Margaret A. Rowe

Library of Congress Catalog Card Number: 68–14331

Printed in Great Britain

Preface

THIS BOOK is an attempt to portray New Zealand as it is today without exaggerating either its strengths or its weaknesses. In order to do this a historical perspective has been given along with a description of the country's physical characteristics and its social and economic structure.

It is easy to over-write New Zealand's scenic attractions and social experiments. While these are characteristics, it is equally important to capture the intimacy of life in a small country such as New Zealand and the luxury of uncrowded living.

Our grateful thanks are due to the Alexander Turnbull Library and the Tourist and Publicity Department for supplying photographs and to the Lands and Survey Department for supplying maps. Thanks are also due to Professor Joan Stevens of the Victoria University of Wellington for her advice and encouragement, and to all our friends for their patience under interrogation.

Wellington   J. W. R.
July 1967   M. A. R.

Maps

Contents

9

List of Illustrations

Acknowledgements

ACKNOWLEDGEMENT for kind permission to reproduce illustrations is made to the following bodies, to whom the copyright of the illustrations belongs:

The High Commissioner for New Zealand: 20, 22, 24, 29, 30.

The New Zealand Department for Tourism and Publicity, Wellington, New Zealand: 10, 21, 23, 25, 26, 27, 28, 31, 32, 33.

The Radio Times Hulton Picture Library: 1, 3, 4, 5, 7, 8, 16, 17, 18, 19.

The Alexander Turnbull Library, Wellington, New Zealand: 2, 6, 11, 12, 13, 14, 15.

The Early Settlers' Museum, Dunedin, New Zealand: 9.

Chapter 1

Introduction

N EW ZEALAND is a small country only slightly larger than the United Kingdom and with a population less than that of Scotland. The smallness of the population is accentuated by its wide dispersion over two long, narrow islands. Average income is relatively high, and *per capita* demand is therefore great, but the total market is still very small so that few industries can realise economies of scale, unless they produce mainly for export. Smallness has been a pervasive influence on the country's development, both materially and culturally, but isolation even more so.

The South Pacific islands that make up New Zealand are so far south as to be a convenient staging point for the Antarctic, and Australia is the only sizeable inhabited country for thousands of miles. In the early days of European settlement, Great Britain was months away by sailing vessel and Europe and America are still a long way away, in terms of cost if not of time. Being surrounded by so much water has engendered a feeling of isolation which makes it easy to view world events as distant observers with little or no sense of involvement even when the events bear indirectly on New Zealand. This was understandably so in colonial days as the British Government was from the beginning not interested in the country and assumed responsibility for it with great reluctance. Even now, as an active member of the British Commonwealth and the United Nations, New Zealand feels somewhat out on a limb. Isolation has, of course, some advantages in a troubled world, especially when it is combined with strategic insignificance, but the disadvantages, notably heavy freight and travel costs, are considerable.

However, the feeling of being a long way from the heart of Western civilisation has had more serious consequences than the distance itself. Until recently most postgraduate university and professional study has automatically been done abroad and the majority of writers, musicians and other artists have found it necessary to live in Europe, and latterly America, for long periods in order to obtain the requisite stimulation for creative work, and in many cases they have remained overseas. It is still said that New Zealand is a good place in which to bring up children but a bad place for cultural or scholarly endeavour. In the early years of European settlement the country was able to subsist on the education and taste of its numerous gifted immigrants. Then came the lean period in which most people were too busy for learning or culture and the pull of Great Britain was very strong for those few who did care. Only since World War II has there been a viable New Zealand culture which did not self-consciously look over its shoulder at the 'Old Country'.

Besides being small and isolated, New Zealand is very new. The indigenous inhabitants, the Maoris, probably began arriving about A.D. 1000 although nobody knows the date with any accuracy. European settlers did not appear in any number until after 1840 and the population passed the million mark only this century. (Even now it is well under three million.) Immigration is still substantial and few families can claim more than three generations of residence. Despite its short history as a nation, New Zealand has achieved much materially and something culturally. The people have developed recognisable characteristics, some good, some bad.

Because of the smallness of the country there is an inevitable tendency to think small. Thus the escalation of the war in Vietnam early in 1965 aroused less public interest than a new system of bank charges. However, the subsequent decision to send troops to Vietnam started off a vigorous debate and perhaps for the first time there was a general realisation that the country is of age and responsible for its decisions as well as entitled to make them. Similarly, the prospective entry of the United Kingdom into the European Common Market in 1962 was regarded almost exclusively from the standpoint of its immediate effect on New Zealand. Again, a proposal to site a hydroelectric dam in a trout fishing area provoked more discussion than a ten-year electricity generation plan involving hundreds of millions of pounds. The effect on the small man is the touchstone of most political thinking and the large enterprise, although often demonstrably more efficient, is automatically suspect. The recent spate of company take-overs, for example, is widely condemned despite the moribund nature of the majority of victims.

A small country might be expected to display cohesion between its various parts but this is not the case. The South Island envies the North Island's more rapid progress, Auckland is regarded with suspicion by all other places because of its concentration of population and hence political power, and adjacent boroughs in the same urban area cannot bring themselves to co-operate without pressure from Government. Relations between Government and local authorities are generally strained with the former endeavouring to increase its overall control and the latter trying to secure special concessions. Rivalry between towns sometimes goes to ludicrous lengths, as between two provincial towns a few miles apart which quarrelled violently over which was to have its airport upgraded to take larger aircraft. In the end a special road was constructed to pacify the loser. The pragmatic New Zealand outlook, however, ensures that most internal rivalries have a solid economic basis, such as who is going to pay or how the proceeds are to be shared. Sentiment plays little part.

There is an insular temper in New Zealand and yet the country has played a significant role in two world wars and in the United Nations and other international bodies. New Zealanders hold a surprising number of important positions abroad, in part a reaction against the 'small man' mentality which has led many able people to emigrate to countries where the rewards for energy, skill and enterprise are greater. Some 'brain drain' from so small and isolated a country may be unavoidable but it is greatly assisted by the generally low level of senior administrative and professional salaries. The gap between these and the wages of an unskilled worker is very small by world standards although some departure from egalitarianism is now becoming noticeable. Another factor encouraging the emigration of skills is the high level of personal income tax on all but top incomes. Strangely enough for a country almost obsessed with equality in the past, the maximum rate of tax is much lower than in most Western countries, the main beneficiaries being the self-employed of whom farmers constitute the majority. The absence of any capital gains tax has also greatly benefited owners of capital. The disparity between New Zealand and overseas salaries is, of course, especially serious for positions that are normally open to international competition, such as university posts.

New Zealanders are said to read more books about themselves and their country than any other people. This may well reflect an inferiority complex, for New Zealanders do not have any special sense of destiny as a nation. On the other hand many succumb to the temptation of considering New Zealand more important in world affairs than is really the case. Self-centredness seems to be encouraged by the equable climate and the absence of acute social or economic divisions. There is a widespread smugness that is appropriately summed up in a former Prime Minister's phrase 'God's own country'.

New Zealand, unlike Australia, was fortunate in never being a convict colony. The majority of early settlers were of yeoman British stock and the spirit of independence and self-reliance which they brought with them has largely persisted although in an odd way. The 'Kiwi' (the familiar name for a born New Zealander, derived from a unique indigenous, wingless bird) is not over-impressed by authority, but he is prone to lean on the Government. The seeds of 'the Welfare State' lie deep in the country's history. New Zealanders are not lazy but they frequently display more energy in leisure activities than at work. Concern for principle has never been a national characteristic and pragmatism decides most issues. Thus the definition of politics as the art of the possible finds ready acceptance. The price, of course, is a monochrome society but one where few people get hurt. The country is prosperous and those who wish to make money can do so without much effort and those who do not are looked after by the State.

However, New Zealanders are vulnerable to criticism from overseas. This is shown by the alacrity and petulance with which any criticism is answered, no matter how trivial. It is revealed truth that the country has the highest standard of living in the world. Some would admit that perhaps the United States is ahead but most would still hold that New Zealand makes up for any lack of material comfort by other factors, especially the more equal distribution of wealth. The view that New Zealand is losing out in the international league table has latterly gained some acceptance and there is now more interest in economic growth but this is rather academic as few pressure groups evince any willingness to sacrifice their entrenched positions to assist the process of faster growth.

Another aspect of smugness is the refusal of most people to accept that the country has a racial problem stemming from the rapid increase in Maori population. The lack of jobs in country areas has led to the congregation of Maoris in the main centres, particularly Auckland. There is no legal discrimination between Maoris and pakehas (Europeans) but Maoris find it hard to find jobs and even harder to find suitable accommodation. The controversy some years ago concerning the eligibility of Maoris to tour South Africa as members of a representative rugby team made New Zealanders realise that they must make racial equality a fact, at least in sport. When towards the end of 1965 the Prime Minister of South Africa dropped his bombshell that Maoris would not be welcome in the team to tour that country in 1967, there was a general realisation that this spelt the end of New Zealand-South African rugby. For a country in which both races regard rugby football almost as a religion this was a considerable advance.

At the 1966 Census approximately 7½ per cent of New Zealanders were Maoris. When information on race was first collected in 1916, the proportion was 4½ per cent. This change clearly reflects the relatively rapid growth of the Maori population which today stands at just over 200,000. Although the number of Maoris prior to European settlement is not known with any accuracy, it is probable that they are more numerous now than ever before. Other races still account for only 1½ per cent of the total population but the proportion has risen sharply in this century through both natural increase and immigration.

The comparative homogeneity of the New Zealand people is further emphasised by the predominantly British origin or descent of the European section of the population. No precise measure of this is possible but it is almost certainly over 90 per cent, despite considerable Irish immigration in the past and substantial Dutch immigration more recently. There is thus no great variety in national characteristics although people still claim to detect a Scots dourness in Otago and Southland and an Irish carefreeness on the west coast of the South Island. There are, however, places where the distribution of surnames indicates the non-British origin of the early settlers. Thus Yugoslavian names are relatively common in Northland and Danish names about Dannevirke.

From World War II until a few years ago the birth rate was approximately 26 per 1,000 but it has now fallen to 22 and is apparently still falling. This may be attributed both to the widespread use of oral contraceptives and to a levelling-out of the marriage age after a period of rapid decline. The Maori birth rate has declined along with that of the pakeha population but it is still substantially higher. This is partly a consequence of the relative youthfulness of the Maori population.

At the present time over 70 per cent of New Zealanders live in the North Island – the smaller of the two main islands – compared with barely 50 per cent at the turn of the century. The drift to the north and to a better climate has accelerated in recent years and this has occasioned a good deal of southern misgiving. The more rapid growth of population in the North Island has been concentrated around Auckland and Wellington, the two main cities, and in the country at large the trend is strongly towards the cities. Over three-fifths of the population now live in urban areas. The image of New Zealand as a predominantly farming country is rapidly becoming outmoded. There are no big cities by world standards but there are a large number of provincial centres. The drift of Maoris to the cities is especially notable. In 1961 under 30 per cent of Maoris lived in urban areas; by 1966 the proportion had risen to over 40 per cent.

With a total population of under three million and a land area of over 100,000 square miles, New Zealand has of course a very low density of population. This is one of the pleasant aspects of the country; everyone lives within easy reach of open country and a high proportion of younger people shoot, tramp or climb mountains. Fishing and swimming are possible for almost everyone. The relative absence of pressure on available land is reflected in the abundance of sports grounds and public parks in urban areas, as well as by the small number of apartment houses. Nearly everyone lives in houses on individual lots.

Following twenty years of high birth rates, the population is comparatively young so that the proportion of labour force to population is rising. At the present time roughly 15 per cent of the labour force is engaged in farming and other primary industries, 25 per cent in manufacturing, 10 per cent in building and construction, 10 per cent in transport, communications and utilities, 20 per cent in commerce and 20 per cent in service industries and administration. As in other high-income countries, the trend is for the farming proportion to decline and the services proportion to increase, with manufacturing remaining constant. Although only one person in seven now has anything directly to do with the land it is still the cornerstone of life in New Zealand. The political pre-eminence of the farming community is a thing of the past, but the economic importance of primary industry is as great as ever.

Chapter 2

The Land

NEW ZEALAND has an area of just over one hundred thousand square miles of which about two-thirds is economically useful, the rest being mainly mountains. The country comprises two main islands of nearly equal size separated by a narrow strait, and a number of smaller islands, some of them hundreds of miles away. New Zealand also administers the South Pacific islands of Nuie and the Tokelaus and a sector of the Antarctic continent named the Ross Dependency. The administrative boundaries of New Zealand proper extend from 33° to 53° south latitude and from 162° east to 173° west longitude but most of this vast area is sea.

Australia, over a thousand miles to the north-west, is the nearest land mass. The following distances give an idea of New Zealand's remoteness from the rest of the world – Singapore, Hong Kong and Japan 5,000 miles, the west coast of the United States 6,000 miles, India and South Africa 7,000 miles and the United Kingdom 11,000 miles. The introduction of jets to New Zealand's international air routes has greatly reduced the country's sense of isolation but travel other than between Australia and New Zealand, for which incidentally passports and health certificates are not required, is still a major undertaking and relatively expensive.

Travel within New Zealand can also be very time-consuming, except by air, because of the rugged terrain. Coastal shipping is used only for goods and the railways carry a declining proportion of passengers, partly because numerous narrow tunnels limit the width of rolling stock and thus prevent the operation of fast expresses. The change from steam to diesel locomotives begun in 1956 has enabled some time-saving but the journey from Auckland to Wellington, a distance of some 350 miles, still takes almost 14 hours by Limited Express. There are also bus services linking most cities and towns but again the difficult country to be traversed makes for long journeys. Although New Zealand is highly motorised, the small population has justified the construction of freeways only around the main cities; but roads are good even in rural areas. The last two decades have seen a great expansion of private motoring but an even more spectacular increase in air travel, until today all major centres have airfields served by scheduled air services.

The extreme north of New Zealand, rather unimaginatively called Northland, is atypical of the country as a whole in many respects, including physical characteristics. The land from Auckland, straddling its narrow isthmus, to the tip of the North Island is a low-lying peninsula with a distinctly sub-tropical climate. Kauri trees, relatives of the pine family, once abounded and some have survived the depredations of the early settlers in the sanctuary of forest reserves. Land once covered with kauri forest has proved very difficult to cultivate because the leached soil forms a hard pan and agriculture in Northland cannot be said to flourish even today. The Maori population of Northland is relatively large and a considerable Dalmatian immigration occurred last century. There is only one substantial town in the area – Whangarei – the site of the newly built oil refinery and also of a glass works and a large cement works. Transport has always been a problem which is only now being solved with the upgrading of roads and the construction of airfields. Auckland has for many years been the focus of activity although Kororareka in the Bay of Islands was New Zealand's first capital. Today, Northland is characterised by relatively small dairy farms and by citrus growing. The coastline is very beautiful and fishing, including big-game fishing, is good.

With harbours on both sides and farmlands to north and south, Auckland is strategically situated and not surprisingly it is easily the largest city in New Zealand. The population of the metropolitan area today is over 550,000 and it is currently increasing by 5 per cent a year – two and a half times as fast as the country as a whole. As in other New Zealand cities the population is widely dispersed, most people living in houses on individual sections. This indeed is typical of New Zealand dwellings although high-density apartment houses are becoming more common as urban land values rise. Because of the low population density, the elongated shape of the city and the ubiquity of the private car, public passenger transport in Auckland is steadily declining in popularity. Unlike Wellington, Auckland has never had an effective suburban railway. Passenger ferries still ply across the Waitemata Harbour but the large suburban area served by them is now also linked with the centre of the city by a harbour bridge.

Auckland, with its international airport, has naturally been the point of entry for Polynesian immigrants, especially from Western Samoa and the Cook Islands, and the majority have made their home there. The indigenous Maori population is also large. Auckland is the most cosmopolitan of New Zealand cities and in many respects is Sydney writ small. It has long been the manufacturing centre of New Zealand whereas Wellington is the administrative headquarters. Under construction in Auckland at the present time is the first full-scale steel works which will be based on indigenous iron sands which abound on the west coast of the island, and on coal from nearby open-cast mines. The only sugar refinery, dockyard, gin distillery and aluminium fabricating plant are in Auckland as well as the country's major nylon plant. Generally, the concentration of nearby industry in terms of employment is more than double that of any other centre.

South of Auckland lies the Waikato, a noted dairying area, the provincial mascot for which is Mooloo the cow as opposed to Ferdinand the bull which symbolises Taranaki, the other historic home of dairy farming. The country is low-lying and relatively fertile although no New Zealand soils have much natural fertility. Heavy application of artificial fertilisers, mostly superphosphate, has greatly boosted stock-carrying capacity in recent years. Because of the long-standing shortage of labour, most farms are highly mechanised and employ very little labour. Hamilton, the centre of the Waikato, has a population of over 65,000. It is the home of the first university in New Zealand to introduce integrated Arts degrees spanning several disciplines.

To the south is the rugged and sparsely populated King Country and to the south-west the province of Taranaki, with New Plymouth as its provincial centre. New Plymouth was one of the early organised settlements but its progress was slow until a breakwater was constructed to convert the open roadstead into a safe anchorage for ocean-going vessels. Now it has a population of over 35,000 and is making steady if unspectacular progress. The nearby town of Waitara was the scene of the first battles of the Maori Wars of the 1860's. The most prominent feature of the Taranaki landscape is Mt. Egmont, a regularly-shaped extinct volcano over 8,000 feet in height strongly reminiscent of Mt. Fujiyama in Japan. This area is also notable for the discovery of natural gas in 1959. All earlier attempts to discover petroleum in any quantity have been unavailing but several small oil wells in New Plymouth have been in production for many years. It is proposed to pipe the natural gas discovered in south Taranaki to Auckland and Wellington and to use the condensate set free as a feedstock for the oil refinery at Whangarei. The abundant rainfall has greatly assisted the development of Taranaki as a dairy-farming area. Dairy farms, like other farms in New Zealand, are almost all family owned but the processing of milk is handled co-operatively.

The centre of the North Island is a volcanic plateau surmounted by a trio of volcanoes, all of which still show signs of activity. Mt. Ruapehu, the highest, is over 9,000 feet in height and a very popular ski resort. Thermal activity is present throughout the area but especially about Lake Taupo, the largest lake in the whole country and itself a sunken volcanic crater. A large geothermal power station has been constructed at nearby Wairakei, and at Lake Rotorua to the north geysers and blow holes abound. Rotorua, the main town, has a population of over 30,000 and many of its homes enjoy thermal hot-water systems. The whole Taupo-Rotorua area is famed for its trout fishing. In the vicinity of Rotorua are large man-made forests of radiata pine which is the basis of two large pulp and paper enterprises as well as many sawmills. Just north of Rotorua is the Bay of Plenty, centring on Tauranga, where there are many fine beaches. The Coromandel Peninsula between Tauranga and Auckland is a backwater today but once the area was a world-famous goldfield. Gold was first discovered in New Zealand just as the Klondyke became worked out and Otago in the South Island attracted prospectors from many parts of the world. As this field declined, gold was discovered on the west coast of the South Island and shortly afterwards at the base of the Coromandel Peninsula which proved to be the best goldfield of all. The present population of the Coromandel area is tiny, but abandoned 'ghost' towns are nostalgic reminders of more exciting days when the number of pubs in a settlement indicated the wealth of the diggings. Today, however, gold production is as negligible as kauri gum collecting.

The eastern side of the North Island is sheep-farming country because of its ruggedness and relatively low rainfall but more recently vegetable growing and fishing have assumed considerable importance. Provincial cities of Gisborne, Napier and Hastings are the focal points of the Poverty Bay-Hawkes Bay region. All three cities are

situated on pockets of relatively fertile soil now producing substantial cash crops although the surrounding areas are predominantly
sheep-farming districts. The Poverty Bay region has difficult problems of soil erosion and large areas of predominantly Maori land are
now reverting to bush or being planted in forest.

South of Taranaki is the old-established city of Wanganui and its
more recent but larger and faster growing rival Palmerston North.
The Wanganui district has a great scenic attraction in the Wanganui
River which rises on the slopes of Mt. Ruapehu and travels to the
sea through magnificent bush-clad gorges. The hinterland, however,
has but limited economic potential whereas Palmerston North serves
a rich farming area.

Further south still one reaches Wellington, the capital and second
largest urban area, with a population of nearly 300,000. Wellington
has one of the best natural harbours in the world, likened by many
to San Francisco. The city is also noted for its winds which blow
most of the time, either from the north or the south. Wellington
proper is very hilly with many houses perched on precipitous slopes,
but the superb views compensate for the inconvenience of mountain-
goat life. The adjacent Hutt Valley, on the other hand, is a fertile
river flat nestling between steep hills. Right down one side of the
Hutt Valley and Wellington Harbour and through some of the
suburbs is a pronounced fault line. Minor earthquakes are common
and a considerable part of Wellington's commercial area is built
on land thrown up as recently as 1855 by a major earthquake.
Fortunately, no serious loss of life has been experienced in Wellington, unlike Napier which was virtually razed by an earthquake in
1931. The development of Wellington has been hindered by its
limited hinterland, the difficult land access and shortage of suitable
building sites. There is large-scale manufacturing in the Hutt Valley
but very little in the capital proper.

Roll-on roll-off ferries connect Wellington, via Cook Strait, with
Picton, the northern terminal of the South Island railway system.
Picton is a little town at the head of a sunken valley, one of a
complex of sounds. The north-eastern part of the South Island is a
sparsely populated sheep-farming area with no large towns. To the
west is the small city of Nelson with its hinterland of hops, tobacco,
orchards and small-scale farming. The population of the South
Island as a whole is growing very slowly and that of the northern
part hardly at all.

An actual population decline is occurring in Westland, cut off from the rest of the island by the Southern Alps through which there are few passes. In its hey-day during the gold rush of the 1860's Westland was a hive of activity with a population many times the present level. The plain between the Alps and the sea is narrow, the rainfall is heavy and large areas of land have been ruined by gold dredges — the last of which ceased operation only a few years ago. Farming in this area is marginal and coalmining, once a major activity, has seriously declined in recent years, but timber milling is assuming greater importance.

Christchurch, with the rich Canterbury plains beyond, is prosperous and growing quite rapidly with a present population of a quarter of a million. There is considerable manufacturing activity in and around Christchurch. A road tunnel and a rail tunnel connect Christchurch with the adjacent port of Lyttelton but a lot of goods traffic is now carried to and from the North Island by rail, using the inter-island ferries for the Picton–Wellington part of the journey. Car and passenger ferries link Lyttelton with Wellington directly.

The Canterbury plains have long been the main wheat-growing area of New Zealand and the foothills of the Alps behind them is excellent sheep country. The plains are the only part of New Zealand where there is much cash crop farming. Elsewhere pasture-livestock farming is the rule with crops only to provide off-season pasture supplementation. In this respect as well as others, Canterbury, and particularly Christchurch, retain a peculiarly English flavour. The presence of the Anglican Cathedral in the middle of the city square symbolises this characteristic.

Further south lies Dunedin, New Zealand's fourth city, with over 100,000 people. It retains a characteristic flavour which, like that of Christchurch, dates back to its original settlement. Once easily New Zealand's leading city, it is today almost static. Dunedin's early growth owed much to the Otago gold rush of the 1860's but the relative poorness of the country behind it has finally blighted its prospects. Appropriately in view of its Scottish heritage, the University looms larger in Dunedin than in any other New Zealand city. Otago University has a medical school, a dental school and a school of mining and metallurgy as well as all the usual faculties. There is also a school of physical education and a large theological college attached to the University.

The remaining substantial New Zealand city is Invercargill, right at the bottom of the South Island and the centre of a prosperous fat lamb farming area. A large hydro-electric development scheme is under way to the north aimed at producing enough power for a possible aluminium smelter. Southland has a well deserved reputation for efficient farming and Bluff, the port of Invercargill, was the first to install all-weather loading facilities. Across Foveaux Strait from Bluff is Stewart Island, almost entirely covered in native bush to this day. Foveaux Strait produces good mud oysters although Aucklanders maintain that their rock oysters have a more delicate flavour.

Besides the main cities there are small villages and market towns throughout the country. Some of these settlements are very small, consisting of a tiny school, a post office cum store and a bus stop or railway station. In dairying areas, the co-operative dairy factory is the main centre of activity. Often there is a community hall, built as a memorial to the First or Second World War, and a small church of one denomination or another. Very few of these settlements have much, if any, aesthetic appeal; even the larger market centres have a main street uniformity very depressing to a newcomer.

Four hundred odd miles to the east of New Zealand proper are the Chathams, a low-lying, windswept group of islands with a population of under 500 today — mainly of Maori origin. It was once considered that this was the last haven of Polynesian precursors of the Maoris — the Morioris — but it is now thought that the original Chatham Islanders were an early group of Maoris possibly blown off course or driven there by later waves of immigrants.

Since the combined length of the two main islands is over 1,000 miles and both are elongated, New Zealand has a very long coastline in relation to its area but the country is poorly endowed with natural harbours — at least where they are economically useful. Auckland and Wellington, the two main ports of the North Island, are exceptionally fine harbours but in the South Island the only good natural anchorage of any economic value is Queen Charlotte Sound at the northern tip. The mountainous nature of much of the country has made land transport very difficult and many ports have been artificially developed either by dredging or constructing breakwaters (to counteract high seas and ocean drifts that cause shoaling at river mouths and harbour entrances).

Apart from the low-lying peninsula in the extreme north, the New

Zealand land mass is distributed along a north-easterly–south-westerly axis formed by the main mountain chains. The rugged nature of New Zealand is one of its striking physical characteristics. The North Island landscape is dominated by many volcanic peaks but there are also several systems of fold mountains. Only a quarter of the land surface lies below the 650-foot contour and much of the higher ground is unusable because of its height or deep indentations. The South Island is even more mountainous but there is little evidence of any volcanic activity. The Southern Alps, with Mt. Cook (12,349 feet) as the highest peak, run along much of the island, close to the west coast. This massive range with no fewer than sixteen peaks higher than 10,000 feet is flanked on the east by smaller ranges. Associated with the Southern Alps is an extensive glacier system flowing on both sides. The glaciers on the western side are shorter, steeper and faster. They are important tourist attractions while those on the eastern side are also economically useful as they feed an extensive river and lake system utilised for irrigation and the generation of electricity.

The economic development of the South Island has been greatly affected by its extensive mountain network. Communication by land between east and west coasts is still difficult, whereas the mountains of the North Island do not create transport problems to anything like the same extent. The prevailing westerly winds lead to heavy rainfall on the western slopes of the Southern Alps and consequently dry conditions in the plains of Canterbury and the plateaus of Otago where the existence of large areas of elevated open country has encouraged large-scale pastoral farming. The mountains of the North Island have much less effect on climatic conditions and the rainfall is more even. For this reason the North Island was heavily wooded in its natural state, whereas large parts of the South Island were never afforested.

New Zealand has many rivers but most are swift flowing with sand bars at their mouths. They are therefore almost useless for commercial purposes; indeed most are too dangerous for pleasure craft. As sources of electricity, however, they are most important. Historically, they also assisted the development of the country because over a hundred years ago the beds of many South Island rivers were found to contain extensive alluvial gold deposits. Today, together with most New Zealand lakes, they are notable for their trout fishing. The largest lake, Taupo, in the middle of the North Island volcanic plateau, is 1,172 feet above sea level and utilised for hydro-electricity via a series of dams and generating stations on the country's largest river, the Waikato.

New Zealand is a small country but its geological history is as complex as that of a continent. There must have been land in the area from the oldest Palaeozoic times or earlier, although little of the country was above sea level at the end of the Tertiary period. Long periods of gradual change through gentle warping and denudation were interrupted by great spasms of mountain building when earth stresses quickly altered the whole configuration of the land. In the Pleistocene period there was also considerable volcanic activity in the North Island and this continues today, New Zealand being part of the unstable Circum-Pacific Mobile Belt characterised by active volcanoes and mountain building. Earthquake activity is comparable with that of California but much less than for Japan or Chile. The last earthquake involving any major loss of life occurred in 1931.

The main influences on New Zealand's climate are the prevailing westerly winds, the country's isolation from other land masses and its rugged terrain. Extreme variations in temperatures do not occur and rainfall is relatively well spread and high on average. The prevailing winds passing over the south-west–north-east chain of mountains result in relatively high rainfall on the west coast and much greater climatic differences from west to east than from north to south. For a large part of the country rainfall is spread fairly evenly throughout the year. Nearly everywhere it averages 25–60 inches a year, a range favourable to plant growth in the temperate zone.

Mean temperature at sea level ranges from 59° Fahrenheit in the north to 49°F in the south. The highest temperatures are experienced east of the main ranges where they rise above 90°F on a few days of the year. The highest and lowest temperatures ever recorded anywhere are 101°F and −3°F. In northern and western districts the difference between summer and winter average temperatures is 15°F reaching a maximum of 25°F in central Otago, the only part of the country with anything resembling a continental climate. Excluding central Otago and inland Canterbury, where heavy frosts occur, winters are mild and pastures maintain continuous growth. Throughout the country sheep and cattle remain in the open all the year round. Most New Zealanders see snow only on the mountains. Humidity is commonly between 70 and 80 per cent in coastal areas

and 10 per cent lower inland. Only in Northland are humid mid-
summer conditions at all oppressive but even there temperatures
rarely reach 85°F. The eastern parts of the North Island and the
northern tip of the South Island are the sunniest parts of New
Zealand. A large part of the country enjoys at least 2,000 hours of
sunshine a year and the sun shines often even in winter. The climate
is thus very suitable for human habitation and, indeed life of any
sort. Despite this, there were no animals on the islands of New
Zealand before human settlement, which probably accounts for the
remarkably abundant plant life found by the Maoris when they
arrived. It is unfortunately certain that the animals introduced by
the white man made inroads into the native forest. Known as 'bush'
by New Zealanders, native forest has unique characteristics setting it
apart from any other vegetation in the world. Because the country
was isolated from early geological times, a large number of plant
species developed which are peculiar to New Zealand. Within some
genera there also took place a remarkable development of species, as
well as considerable hydridisation. It is interesting that New Zealand
possesses few of the main Australian genera, though some of its
natives are akin to plants found in South Africa, South America and
Malaya. Another important characteristic of New Zealand bush is
the number of plants with distinctive juvenile and mature forms.
The country's wide range of latitude and altitude permits many
varieties of plant life, from the mangroves found in sub-tropical
swamp conditions in the north, to the numerous alpine species growing above the snow line of New Zealand's mountain chain.

The original forest consisted mostly of a lush broadleaf growth
which is almost completely evergreen. The forest floor was tightly
packed with many different species of ferns and mosses and the trees
themselves were so hung with lianas and epiphytic plants that the
bush was almost impenetrable and very sombre. Towards the coast,
the broadleaf forest was modified considerably and sturdier, salt-
resistant shrub-trees like the ngaio, the pohutukawa and the kohekohe
appeared at the outer fringe, giving way in their turn to an amazing
array of divaricating shrubs capable of growing and thriving on cliff
faces and beach margins. Further inland this broadleaf forest was
frequently interspersed with podocarps—totara, rimu, miro and
kahikatea—and in the north, kauri—a species of pine tree. These are
all fine timber trees because of the great length of trunk before the
branches appear. The kauri also secretes a beautiful gum. This sort

of bush has largely vanished, giving way to the demands of European settlement for cleared land and high quality timber. Pockets do remain, however, and many of these are now reserves. With an increase in altitude, the broadleaf forest becomes mixed with beech, but a pure stand of beech forest is rare, especially in the North Island.

One peculiar feature of the New Zealand bush is its lack of colour. A dark olive green overall, it requires detailed observation to reveal the subtle changes in texture and light which make it an exciting part of the landscape. Most of the flowering trees and shrubs produce small white or green-white flowers very difficult to see in the subdued light of the forest. Some exceptions to this are the orange-red pohutukawa, flowering in December along the coast and near lakes, the deep red rata in the depths of the bush and the golden kowhai. Even the native orchids are not highly coloured and the alpines do not follow the characteristic colours of their species in other countries. New Zealand has many species of gentians, none of them the brilliant blue found in gentians elsewhere. One of the most notable alpines, *Ranunculus lyalii*, has cream flowers which are made conspicuous by their size, their profusion and the glossy green leaves of the plant. Even the alpine bluebell has a fragile white bell only faintly touched with blue. Many plants, however, have quite brilliant berries, red, black, orange or purple, which appear in the autumn.

The Maoris were very knowledgeable about the plant life of their country, and most plants have Maori names. The bush was precious to them for religious as well as practical reasons and they tried to maintain the ecological balance necessary to keep the bush regenerating.

New Zealand was well served by its first botanists, mostly explorers or missionaries, and it is impossible to praise too highly the scientific perspicacity of these men in their task of systematising the strange and novel plant life confronting them. Of the early men, Bidwill, Hooker and the missionary Colenso perhaps made the most outstanding contributions, Colenso's being all the more remarkable as he was largely self-taught. Later, Cheesman, Allan and Cockayne carried out work on New Zealand flora which was internationally recognised and honoured. Cockayne was a particularly important figure in that he recognised some considerable time before botanists in other parts of the world the tremendous importance of plant ecology.

The people of New Zealand had a great deal to learn from this discovery. The early settlers found that milling and systematic cutting of the bush were methods too slow to clear enough land for farming; they accordingly fired the bush, and burnt off many acres of forest, particularly in the King Country area. As soon as the ashes cooled, they planted grass seed. The experiment was not an unqualified success, although it appeared so at the time. Many of the burnt areas were very steep – probably steeper than the settlers themselves realised – and the heavy rains which are common throughout New Zealand washed the top soil down into the streams at the bottom of the gullies before the grass could effectively establish itself. Without the roots of the trees to hold the soil, the earth began to slip and a tragic amount of fertile soil was carried down to the sea. The hills were left bare, with great scars of clay and rock exposed to further weathering. With the bush went also the birds, important natural pollinators and seed carriers. The natural cycle had been completely disrupted and it has taken many years of constant effort to fix slipping hillsides with fast growing exotic trees. Some farms in hogback country had to be abandoned and this land has been slowly taken over and restored by the returning bush.

The animals introduced by the European have not helped bush regeneration. Incidentally, the Maoris brought with them only two animals, a rat – the kiore – and a type of dog, the kuri. The rat flourished and is still extant, but life was always a struggle for the kuri, and it died out soon after the arrival of Europeans. Neither of these upset the ecological balance to any significant extent. The early settlers brought with them domestic animals, game animals and animals such as the rabbit which served as a sentimental reminder of home. These species nearly all flourished and multiplied beyond belief; in doing so many of them have become widespread pests.

Red deer were introduced soon after the settlers arrived, and there are now several million head living in herds in hill country areas. Their habit is to browse from the greenery as high as they can reach and also to eat the tender young shoots of tree seedlings and new ferns as they appear on the forest floor. The presence of deer or wild pigs in any number leaves the floor of the bush stripped bare of its normal luxuriant carpet, the nursery of the next generation of trees. Since deer also do great damage to high country pastures, the Government now employs deer hunters in an attempt to control the increasing numbers. There are several other varieties of deer in New

Zealand, including the American elk deer, or wapiti, found only in the Fiordland National Park, where it is hunted for sport.

The Australian opossum was brought to New Zealand with the idea of starting a skin trade. Unfortunately, the animal so enjoyed the conditions it found that today there are few parts of New Zealand without it. Like deer, opossums also do great damage to the bush, being natural canopy browsers who are willing to eat anything young, green and tender. They are curiously bold animals and frequently live close to human settlements – there are many living in the scrub and trees of the capital city's steep banks – where they do considerable damage to fruit crops and gardens. Although opossums were trapped for their skins, it proved quite impossible to control the numbers; at the present time the damage done by the animal appreciably outweighs the value of its skin. The opossum has been declared a 'noxious animal' and local rabbit boards have been asked to help eliminate it altogether.

In New Zealand, as in Australia, the rabbit found its paradise. Introduced by the early settlers for sentimental reasons, the rabbit immediately took to an environment which provided plenty to eat and where the only predator was the odd hawk or the farmer's dog. Rabbits multiplied at an alarming rate, riddling alike the farmer's pasture and the native tussock with countless burrows. They ate the new grasses provided for stock, thus exposing the country to further soil erosion. As early as 1876 efforts were made to control their increase, but real progress was made only when it was decided to exterminate them completely. Even now, the 'last' rabbit is still alive and will probably remain so in spite of poisoning programmes. In 1962, the country spent over one million pounds on rabbit control to prevent any large-scale 'come-back'.

Because of its isolation from other land masses since early geological time, New Zealand had no indigenous animals. Even the lizard family is represented by only two of the world's twenty species. One of these, however, is of considerable interest; young geckos being born alive instead of being hatched from previously laid eggs as happens elsewhere in the world. The tuatara lizard, on the other hand, is quite a different vertebrate. It is the world's only extant example of a 'beak-headed' reptile, which, authorities are agreed, lived about 200 million years ago in the northern continents and became extinct there at least 100 million years ago. Once the tuatara was found throughout New Zealand, but now lives only on outlying islands. It is quite harmless, and lives among coastal shrub. It grows very slowly all its life, finally reaching a length of about two feet, taking about twenty years to become sexually mature and living to well over 100 years.

Like the tuatara lizard, New Zealand's few native frogs are unique to the country. They belong to a genus which features more primitive development of the skeleton and anatomy than that found in any other frog in the world. The presence in New Zealand of these lizards and frogs gives rise to much tantalising speculation about the country's geological history.

However, if there was no land connection to allow animals on to the islands, at least the sea did not prevent birds from reaching them. The Maoris found the forests full of bird life and birds became an important part of their diet. For obvious reasons there were few land birds, but of these, two are extraordinarily interesting. The moa and the kiwi, both wingless birds, must have arrived either by flight, before they lost their wings, or else, as seems most probable, by land, and New Zealand was last in contact with land something like 70 million years ago. The kiwi and the moa have both an immensely ancient lineage. The moa was a very large bird, originally living in all three islands. He was very easily killed by the Maoris, however, and the very big moa probably became extinct soon after A.D. 1000, though smaller bush moas survived for nearly five hundred years after. Moa fossils have been found throughout the country.

On the other hand the kiwi, which belongs to the same family as the moa, is still extant though hardly common. A nocturnal bird, it is rarely seen, but there are quite flourishing colonies in isolated bush areas and even on the fringes of rough farming country. There are other flightless birds in New Zealand – the weka and the takahe (which only just survived the troubles of European occupation) – but these probably became flightless after their arrival. Indeed, a relative of the weka and takahe, the swamp hen, known to the Maoris as 'pukeko', still has wings although it does not often use them.

The native wrens and the New Zealand 'wattle birds' – the huia, saddleback and kokako – and the native thrush all belong to families peculiar to this country. Most of the remaining birds, however, the tui, the fantail, the bellbird and many others, are all closely related to Australian birds. Some Australian birds have even migrated within European memory and seem to have taken up a permanent abode here.

There are many sea birds around New Zealand waters; some are residents but others are migrants, especially from the Antarctic. The predatory skua arrives in summer to take advantage of its Antarctic companions, the petrels, penguins and shags, which have come to the warmer climate to nest. Penguin are quite common, although they are mostly found along the southern coastline and around Stewart Island. Probably the most exciting sub-Antarctic birds, the great albatross, together with other members of the albatross family, live and breed on and about the southern outlying islands of New Zealand – the Chathams are the home of the northern variety, and Campbell Island of the royal albatross. A small breeding colony of royal albatross is also found in the Otago Harbour.

The gannet is a bird which comes from Australia to breed in large colonies in numerous nurseries around New Zealand. The largest gannetry is at Cape Kidnappers where many thousands of pairs hatch and rear their young before returning to Australia. There are also many gulls and terns around the coasts and shags of one variety or another are a common sight in harbours or estuaries, 'hanging out their wings' to dry after they have been fishing.

The sea waters of New Zealand abound with fish, an important factor in the diet of the Maori and of considerable economic interest to the present-day inhabitants of the country. Because New Zealand is the centre of a complex of warm and cool ocean currents, the variety of fish found in the region is unusually great. The warm currents encourage migrations of such tropical species as tuna, marlin and some big game sharks. Local inhabitants of the warm drifts are snapper, trevally and kawahai. The colder currents from the Antarctic, on the other hand, support a different sort of fishing, blue and red cod and hake. However, nearly half of the fish species found around New Zealand are able to live within a considerable range of water temperature. These fish are found practically the whole length of New Zealand's coastline – teraki, groper and bass. Flounder and sole are plentiful along the mudflats of some tidal rivers and in many estuaries and harbours. Crayfish are also found in substantial numbers in many rocky areas of the coastline.

New Zealand has an enormous number of different shellfish, many species unique to the country because of the long period of separation from any other land mass. The Maoris knew the value of shellfish as food and some varieties are also considered great delicacies by Europeans. Opinion is divided about the gourmet qualities of pipis (dug from sand and silt just above low tide level), mussels and paua (prised from rock surfaces). The paua has a most beautiful shell shot with iridescent blues and greens and is frequently used for decorative purposes. It is very common and discarded shells can be picked up along many beaches. However, the toheroa is certainly the finest shellfish the country offers for culinary purposes. A delicacy appreciated by Maori and pakeha alike, it is a clam which burrows itself deep into sandy beaches where there are many sand dunes. New Zealand possesses many beaches backed by sand dunes, but the toheroa confines itself to a select few, in particular, the Ninety Mile Beach, north of Auckland, and the west coast beach of Levin, near Wellington. Toheroa are heavily protected, and a close season is now well established with a limit catch.

Chapter 3

In the Beginning

N EW ZEALAND history consists of three firmly interwoven threads. The strongest and the one on which the others depend is the land itself. The land, its yield and its ownership, have been the main preoccupations of both Maori and European settlers.

The second great thread is the fact that two distinctive peoples arrived to settle and become New Zealanders. Racial relationships have developed uniquely in New Zealand mostly because the Maoris are an intelligent and adaptable people and because the country was settled by Europeans of British stock. Very much influenced by an evangelical humanitarian outlook, these immigrants were prepared to believe, in theory if not always in practice, that the native inhabitants had their own dignity and rights as human beings. This combination did not prevent racial misunderstandings, bitterness and war, but it gave racial strife in New Zealand a character quite different from that in, say, South Africa and the United States.

The third great thread of New Zealand history and one which has emerged most obviously in this century is the development of the Welfare State which seems to the outsider a peculiar and often distasteful fact of national life. This dependence on the State has its roots as far back in the story as the struggle for land, and the need for two races to live together as amicably and with as much dignity as possible. The land, race relations and dependence on the State are the main elements of New Zealand history. They are the forms of the design which the events of history weave and twist in ever-changing patterns.

The land itself is the beginning. Once upon a time before things were as we now know them Papa the earth, the mother of the gods, lay in a warm and close embrace with Rangi the sky, the father of the gods. Of their great affection, Papa conceived and bore many offspring who lay with their parents in the warm darkness. As the god-children grew and increased they felt a great yearning towards

37

light, the exact opposite of that crowded darkness in which they lived. So they conspired together, wondering whether they should kill Papa and Rangi or merely tear them apart from their close embrace. The god of the forest, the father of the trees, Tanemahuta, spoke out that they should use their power to push Rangi the sky afar off, but that they should stay close to the earth, their mother who had suckled them. So they did and when Rangi was torn from his beloved Papa and pushed far off and out, the earth became flooded with light and for the first time they could see. But Tawhiri-ma-tea, the god of the winds and the storms, grieved for his father Rangi and departed with him. Up to this present the heaven has remained separated from his wife, the earth, and greatly they mourn their trouble. The earth grieves for her beloved; her sighs rise up from her mountains and wooded valleys: men call them mists. Heaven weeps gently from his loneliness afar off: men call his tears dewdrops.

And so the gods lived on earth, loving, quarrelling and begetting happily enough. One of the children, Maui the son of Taranga, became a god-man, living and playing with his brothers and sisters among the gods. As he grew older he extracted from the gods their secret powers so that men came to possess fire and the art of making hunting tackle. It was with the fish-hook made from part of the jaw-bone of his grandmother, Muri-ranga-whenua, that Maui fished up the North Island of New Zealand, Te Ika a Maui, the fish of Maui. But the hero died trying to steal the gift of immortality from his ancestress, Hine nui-te-po.

The Maoris are a Polynesian people and thus they explained the creation of the world. Their legends claim that they themselves came to New Zealand from Hawaiki (perhaps the Society Islands) as a result of an earlier exploration by Kupe, who visited New Zealand and returned to tell them of the marvels awaiting them. After a considerable lapse of time a mighty fleet of canoes set sail and, with the direct purpose of emigration, followed Kupe's navigating directions until after an heroic hardship-riven voyage they reached New Zealand. There are other theories about how the Maoris reached New Zealand, so far to the south of the other Polynesian groups. The Polynesians could navigate from island to island but they never undertook transoceanic voyages like the Vikings. It seems most probable that the Maoris reached the country by accident, being blown off course on fishing expeditions or inter-island voyages.

Certainly they never attempted to sail back, or were unsuccessful if they did, and it seems unlikely that they would easily lose such a sophisticated skill as that of deliberate oceanic navigation. Lacking any certain evidence, however, one theory seems as good as another, a topic for perpetual anthropological speculation, against which must always be set the strong legendary tradition, found among all the Maoris, of the journey of the great fleet. The names of the canoes and those who arrived in them form the beginning of the Maori table of genealogy from which was often deduced claims for land.

The Maoris lived mainly in the North Island, where they used almost the whole island to support themselves. The dense bush with which the North Island was largely covered was treated with great care. It yielded wood for houses, for palisades to protect the pa or tribal collection of houses, for canoes and other necessities. There were no indigenous animals but many wingless birds. The largest of these, the moa, ranged in herds across the plains of the South Island and the Maoris soon killed them all, they were so large and defence-less. The Maoris lived on fish, birds, tree roots and berries, and the kumara, a sweet potato which they had brought with them. They lived an active well-ordered existence with a complicated system of law and religion administered by the ariki, the chief of the tribe, and the tohunga, the priest. The Maoris had an advanced stone age culture; their techniques with tools were well developed and their ability to ornament canoes, meeting houses and implements was of a surprising sophistication. Much of their carving was of exquisite intricacy and obviously depended on a careful and accurate observa-tion of natural forms and patterns: the unrolling of a fern leaf, the wave pattern left on the sand by the retreating tide, the whorl of a seashell. The whole structure of Maori society was very carefully regulated and based upon the rhythm of a subsistence livelihood, but yet with enough leisure to explore, ornament, compose poetry and play stick games very similar to those found in other Polynesian islands. The climate of New Zealand is cooler than that of more northerly islands so the Maoris generally showed considerably more energy in their daily life than other Polynesian races and always in the summer there was the entertainment of an intertribal war to avenge an injury or to acquire a coveted fishing right. Maoris were also occasional cannibals – probably when protein foods were scarce.

It was to this well established and isolated society that Abel Tasman's two vessels made a brief appearance in 1642. His ships came upon the west coast of the South Island and, in attempting to make friendly overtures to the native inhabitants, he lost four of a boat's crew. He fired upon the Maoris from his ship, but left them the undoubted victors of round one. He then sailed north for home, assessing the Maoris as a bad prospect for trade, decidedly hostile, and the land itself perhaps the edge of that fabulous land of Beach, the great continent of 'Southland'. The next European visitor was James Cook in 1769. His remarkably accurate charts of two large islands dispelled hopes of the Southland continent, and his detailed observations of the country altered the whole course of its history. Again the explorer was met with violence. In the North Island, near the present city of Gisborne, a hostile native was killed and later more Maoris were killed in a canoe when they had become un- comfortably aggressive. However, the Maoris were not to be easily frightened and generally speaking Cook found them ready to be friendly and eager to trade. Cook in his later voyages estimated the country as good for European occupation, with a temperate climate capable of growing most European crops. He was impressed with the intelligence of the Maoris and also with the quality of the timber and flax they had to sell. Commercial exploitation was an obvious result of the publication of his report in the *Journal* in 1777.

The detailed completion of Cook's charts was made by a number of explorers and notably by a small party of Frenchmen. One of these, Dumont d'Urville, was a valuable recorder of Maori life. Other French expeditions, the arrival of a French missionary bishop and a colonising attempt, gave substance to the later fear that New Zealand might become a French colony. Mostly, however, people who were attracted to the country in the late eighteenth and the early nineteenth centuries were sealers and whalers who made their headquarters down in the south. Men also came for the long lengths of timber produced by many native trees, and for the flax which they bartered from the Maoris. Mostly the Maoris were friendly, and willingly provided the labour to load the ships, but sometimes they coveted and stole the white man's goods. Then relations became violent, not always to the Maoris' disadvantage. As the century wore on, more and more whaling ships arrived from the eastern seaboard of the United States and a small settlement grew up at Russell in the Bay of Islands. Here gathered escaped convicts from Sydney and the flotsam and jetsam from the whaling ships as well as honest traders. Always the Maoris were learning; they liked beads, rugs, pretty vanities, axes, muskets and liquor. Generally speaking, New Zealand was an ungentle and lawless place, notorious throughout the southern hemisphere and beyond.

Into this atmosphere came Samuel Marsden, an evangelical Anglican missionary from Sydney. He had been shocked by the tales of licence which had reached him in Sydney and appalled to hear of the Maoris making war upon each other with the guns they acquired from the traders. Not a well educated man, Marsden was full of fervour for his calling, believing that as well as the religion of the white man, the Maori must also be taught to conform to his society and way of living. He therefore took with him to New Zealand a school teacher and two artisans to teach the natives the skilled crafts of carpentry, shoe making and rope making. On Christmas Day 1814 in the Bay of Islands Marsden preached the Gospel in New Zealand for the first time from the text 'Behold I bring you good tidings of great joy'. Then he left, leaving his three catechists to a dispiriting and dreary task.

Marsden's mission could not be called a brilliant success, but it marked the beginning of the missionaries. Soon there were Methodists as well as Anglicans in the field, followed shortly after by Bishop Pompallier, a Roman Catholic. In terms of the conversion rate, the efforts of these well-meaning, pious men went unrewarded for a surprising length of time, but the Maori was very eager to acquire from them any European skills which they could impart. Coming from an overwhelmingly humanitarian climate, the missionaries were sure that the English way of living, its manners and codes, was the only Christian way. To be a Christian it was necessary to dress like an Englishman. Reasonably enough, the Maoris were reluctant overnight to become Europeans in the name of a religion for which they could not see the need. However, when their language had been given an alphabet, and prayer books and the Bible in Maori were laboriously produced, the example of the initial and hesitant Maori Christians was soon followed by many others. The great drawback about the mission was the Maori's inexorable logic over the law of love, the message brought to him by white people who could not even maintain peace among themselves. And it was true enough that the settlement in the Bay of Islands was the Achilles heel of any preaching the missionaries might do. They were very conscious that it had become a drunken, brawling disgrace, and after much agitation the British Government

reluctantly agreed that it must provide some sort of unofficial law
and order in a country whose sovereignty was unclaimed but whose
inhabitants were mostly of British origin. In 1833 James Busby
accordingly arrived to take up his position as the British Resident.
His presence had some influence on the rioting in the Bay of Islands,
but both his power and his calibre were inadequate for the task.

The British Colonial Office could not ignore the increasing
number of British subjects in New Zealand, nor, under constant
evangelical and humanitarian pressures in the House of Commons,
could it ignore the troubles which unscrupulous merchants were
visiting upon the unsuspecting natives of the country. On these two
grounds, the fact of occupation and the desire to protect the Maoris,
William Hobson, R.N., was sent in 1840 to make an annexing treaty
with the Maoris. The Treaty of Waitangi was more a statement of
goodwill on both sides than a legal treaty: in fact it has no standing
in international law at all. Yet it firmly symbolised, for both races,
the path their combined history was to take. Hobson promised the
Maori chiefs (in effect his agents hawked the treaty throughout the
major North Island tribes) to deal fairly with them, appointed a
protector to guard their welfare and guaranteed their rights to the
land. He provided that all European land titles should derive from
the Crown, which would be the sole purchaser of the land (thus
protecting the Maoris from defrauding Europeans). The Maoris on
their side understood little of the technicalities of the treaty, nor its
broad implications, but they did understand the rights which it was
proposing to uphold, and in signing, they agreed to trust its spirit.
The Treaty of Waitangi begins the formal history of New Zealand.
The State, intervening because there was no one else to do so,
endeavoured to frame a policy, especially with regard to land,
which would enable both races to live and develop peacefully together. The Maoris granted the Queen their sovereignty and Hobson
established himself at Auckland as Governor of the Colony.

His hand was forced, however, by a colonising interest in England
which had for some time been considering New Zealand as the
object of serious settlement following a systematic pattern. Edward
Gibbon Wakefield was an able and ingenious man whose interest in
colonising activities had been quickened by his work in Canada on
the Durham Report. Although unacceptable himself for personal
reasons (he had abducted an heiress and served his time in Newgate
for this social misdemeanour), he had the ear of powerful men in the

House of Commons, and backed by some financiers, he established the New Zealand Company. This body aimed to buy land from the Maoris; sell it at a fairly high price to men of wealth and position who would pay labouring-class immigrants to develop it, and use the profit to finance new immigrant labourers. Wakefield considered that this system would produce a rounded society, encompassing men from all walks of life, in which land, labour and wealth would be delicately balanced.

The only real drawback was that the British Government could not be persuaded to embrace the scheme and when the impatient investors in England heard that New Zealand was finally to become a Crown Colony they sent off a hasty messenger with orders to buy up as much land as possible – a matter of hard cash to beat the official gun. While Hobson was collecting signatures for his Treaty in Auckland, the New Zealand Company's agent was buying land from the Maoris as fast as he could in the south of the North Island. Lacking any idea of the system of tribal holding, the Company bought land from individual Maoris. Often the land was unsuitable and also there were to be years of trouble before the claims of ownership could be more or less established. Hard upon the heels of the buying agent came the immigrants. Wakefield might have dreamed a dream, but his investors certainly concerned themselves mainly with profit. Most of the investors remained in England – absentee landholders – but some actually took up their land. These were educated men and they played an enormous part in the developing country's future. More often than not they were the only people capable of giving a lead in strange, remote and sometimes hostile surroundings. But the blind haste with which Wanganui, New Plymouth, Nelson and Wellington were all settled in the 1840's led to much distress and discontent. There were no jobs waiting for the labourers when they arrived and much of the land purchased had not been surveyed. Instead of a balanced, organised society, these settlements did well to subsist at all.

Although the Company agents had not been over-fastidious in whom they enticed to emigrate (their commission was undoubtedly more important to them than Wakefield's theory), New Zealand was well served by the sturdiness and resourcefulness of the people who came. They were not convicts or criminals and they came, most of them young married couples, to seek a better future than would be theirs in nineteenth-century industrial England. Like Wakefield they too dreamed a dream but their utopia was many a hard year's work away. The great trouble was the question of land titles. In the north, Hobson had promised that all land would be purchased from the Crown. In the south, men were settling on land bought directly from any Maori, without the permission and participation of the other members of the tribe. Everywhere the Maoris found their fishing and hunting rights abruptly ignored as the Company settlers began to establish their farms. In the north Hobson tried to treat the Maoris reasonably but in the south their claims were ignored, and the Governor in Auckland was too far off to worry the settlers. The settlers were vitally interested in buying land — it was, after all, the foundation of their livelihood and interest in the country. The Maoris were interested in selling land, but only up to a point. Their fishing rights, their forestry rights and their custom of tapu (a sacred ban which the priest could place over any area) made them effective, if often invisible, occupiers of large tracts of land which were all held tribally. Hobson endeavoured to buy up as much land in the north as he could, but he had little or no control over the agents of the New Zealand Company, illegally buying land as fast as they could round Wellington and New Plymouth.

With such a tremendous demand for land it became more and more important that the Crown held to its right to be the only purveyor of land to the settlers. To prevent speculation and exploitation of the Maoris, the Crown insisted on its right to be the sole purchaser from the Maoris but this often led to considerable delays, especially in the south of the North Island, so far from the seat of official Government. In the face of constant pressure from the settlers which increased when the Maoris began to menace infant settlements, Fitzroy, the Governor appointed on Hobson's death in 1842, was incapable of acting with any delicacy. Without effective troops, he was unable to prevent the aggression of the Maoris in the south where Te Rauparaha, whether or not provoked, massacred a surveying party at Wairau. As well as few troops, Fitzroy also had little money. The Crown was unable to buy as much land as the settlers needed, and the Maoris, conscious of their position, were reluctant to sell. Without land, the expanding economy of the small settlements ground to a halt. Fitzroy made a desperate attempt to relieve the position by allowing private settlers to buy land from the Maoris. The unfortunate man was recalled in 1845, being succeeded by George Grey, able, energetic and without the high principles which had in part caused Fitzroy's dilemma. He was a man well understood in the new go-getting colony.

He immediately restored the Crown monopoly on the purchase of Maori land. With greater financial resources at his disposal than his predecessor, he bought Maori land more freely, clearly seeing that the supply of land to be sold must always slightly exceed the number of settlers to buy it. The British Government had also given him more military backing than Fitzroy had had, and with these troops he made a fine showing of power to the southern Maoris, his most effective action in this direction being to kidnap Te Rauparaha under somewhat shady circumstances and hold him in custody until peace and quiet had been restored. With the Maoris he tried to be punctiliously fair in all his negotiations and his purchasing agents were strictly instructed in this direction. Grey had a great respect for the Maoris and their culture, learning their language and collecting their folk-lore. To ensure that they were not exploited, he established what would now be called a department of Maori affairs, with himself firmly in control. He built hospitals and schools in the Auckland province and encouraged the Maoris to develop their land more skilfully, providing them with water mills and any other technical help at his disposal. His great fault was that he did not teach anyone to carry on this aspect of his administration and the cloak of the 'mana' he received from the Maoris was not allowed to descend upon the shoulders of anyone else.

With the settlers he was not quite so successful. They conceded his ability to restore peace and order and to maintain the supply of cheap land which he wished all men to have the opportunity of buying (not just the wealthy as in the Wakefield schemes) but they also bitterly opposed his refusal to operate the 1846 Act giving them self-government. Grey considered the welfare of the Maori safer in his hands than in those of a few thousand white settlers. He did manoeuvre a compromise, however, dividing the country according to the Act into two Provinces and sending a Lieutenant-Governor to live permanently in Wellington. By this time there were six small distinct settlements, all isolated from one another and from the Central Government by a relentless and implacable terrain. The frustration of the settlers produced a consistent outcry from the leading men of Wellington, Nelson, New Plymouth and Canterbury; the Presbyterian Otago settlement was too far south to be relevant and too flourishing to care. The country generally grew bitter about the postponement of adequate self-government. However, in 1852 Grey took a large part in drafting a representative constitution. This provided for six provincial governments and a General Assembly over all.

By 1850 New Zealand's destiny was a European one. There were 25,000 settlers in the country, the whole of the South Island had been purchased from the Maoris and great pastoral expansion was taking place and would continue apace for many years. The North Island had not been so fully bought up because of the large Maori population, and by 1852 the land hunger of an expanding society was becoming so acute that violence was probably inevitable – the more so as Grey had not trained a successor in his policy of positive benevolence towards the Maoris. The 1852 constitution emphasised the European outlook. The franchise was based on a property qualification which gave the vote (or votes, according to the size of the holding) to every male over twenty-one except Maoris. The Governor reserved his rights over Maori relations, but he depended upon finance voted by the General Assembly. The details of local government were dealt with in the Provincial Councils; indeed, the effective government of the colony was carried out by these Councils, and was to be for the next twenty years. The reason for this lay largely in the fact that, under supervision (mostly nominal) of the General Assembly, the Provinces were authorised to sell public lands at whatever price they chose to fix, to settle the size of holdings and to keep the profits. (As in the Wakefield theory, the profits were used to bring out more immigrants.) These land funds proved a bone of contention over which provincial and national interests fought right up to the time of the Maori Wars.

However, by 1856 New Zealand was governed by an elected assembly and administered on a provincial level. The farmlands were expanding as the settlers bit deep into the bush, establishing mixed farms in the North Island, and in the South sheep on the tussock plains well into the rugged foothills of the Alps. Each community formed its own fiercely independent society. The settlers of Canterbury, for example, liked to feel that they were a cut above the other colonists and wished to preserve their superiority at all costs. On the political side, the parochial independence of the small settlements bid fair at times to wreck the slowly developing machinery of government itself. In 1858 C. W. Richmond, of New Plymouth, wrote: 'If Nelson is going to abet the pretensions of

Wellington there is an end to the integrity of the Colony, for which we have been striving. Auckland will not submit to be deposed from her present position, but will demand a lieutenant-governor, which the Home Government has promised. In fact, this Nelson demonstration, if approved of by the constituencies, is nothing less than a breakdown of the Constitution.' In the meantime, however, permanent homes began to appear and primitive make-do huts gave place to something a little better. Life was still very hard but the settlers were their own masters and this made up for many of the comforts left behind in England. For those in the North Island, however, even while prosperity was increasing about them, this was a time of fear and anxiety. While their Provincial Councils haggled over the price of land and the ultimate destiny of the land funds, the Maoris were becoming more and more unsettled and dissatisfied, and there were several small hostile exchanges between settlers and Maoris in the Wanganui and Taranaki areas before the Maori Wars finally broke out.

Their immediate cause was the unwillingness of the Maoris to sell land and the settlers' haste to acquire it. The conflict began with a dispute at Waitara in 1860 and effectively ended with the collapse of Maori resistance in the face of British redcoats in Waikato in 1865, although there were isolated skirmishes for years afterwards. Only the North Island was affected and especially the northern and western parts where there were considerable numbers of both Maoris and settlers. Across the Waitara River, some ten miles from the early settlement of New Plymouth, lay a large tract of Maori land. This was coveted by the hard-pressed settlers of Taranaki, a province which, for one reason or another, had got off to a bad start and was rather conscious of its Cinderella status. Wiremu Kingi (William King), the paramount chief, wished to retain this land in order to provide cohesion for his tribe at a time when European ways were fast displacing Maori customs. He consistently refused to sell to the Government agent and was therefore regarded by the settlers as a bad Maori. A 'good' Maori emerged in the person of a minor chief, Te Teira (Taylor), who offered to sell a small parcel of the land at the mouth of the river; but this was vetoed by Wiremu Kingi, in accordance with Maori custom which Grey had always recognised. The Taranaki settlers, however, had an outspoken champion in the General Assembly, C. W. Richmond, who pressed the Government constantly for more land for settlement in Taranaki.

Governor Gore Browne was well intentioned but weak and quite incapable of resisting the relentless and vocal pressure of the settlers. Forsaking Grey's policy, he announced his intention of buying land from any Maori who could show a sound title to it. This new policy was first expressed in 1860 at New Plymouth, the hot spot of discontent, where the Government agent, Donald McLean, and his local agent must have known of Te Teira's intention to sell tribal property and of the dispute with Kingi.

Again reversing established policy, the Governor refused to countenance Kingi's veto of the sale and Kingi withdrew to fortify his home. The Maori Wars began. For years the two races lived in a state of constant alarm: the settlers riding, fearful and armed, about their farms; the Maoris using every stratagem of bush war-craft to fight a battle which they nearly won, but which they inevitably lost. In Taranaki the war was mostly conducted on a guerrilla basis, but it became a campaign of considerable proportions in the Waikato where again the greed of an outreaching economy clashed with the desperation of the Maori as the values of the missionary proved empty against the claims of wealth. In a way, the Waikato clash was more culpable than the Taranaki outburst where the interplay of personalities led to the final trouble. In the Waikato, it was more directly the hasty greed of the white man which brought war to a large region with a dense Maori population. The Auckland settlers urgently required more land at a reasonable price. The Government had foreseen this demand and had bought up a large area of land just south of Auckland but this had fallen quite cheaply into the hands of speculators who were prepared to hold out for a high price. This block of not-for-sale speculators' land diverted the pressure further south where the large Maori population occupied a big area of rich and fertile land.

However, land negotiations with the Waikato Maoris were complicated by a new factor. Not only were the Maoris efficient farmers, providing a large share of the Colony's exports to Australia, but they had also formed themselves into a sort of politico-mystical union which had tremendous influence among them. It was the first outburst of an organised nationalist feeling and was very largely a leaf taken from the Europeans' own book. From the early 1850's Maori chieftains (and some missionaries) had been alarmed at the inroads of the white frontier. The Maoris were generally prepared to be friendly and helpful but not to the extent of losing their tribal land, which they rightly considered their greatest treasure. While an undercurrent of discontent was gathering way among the Maoris in New Zealand, Te Rauparaha's son visited England. He was received by Queen Victoria and returned impressed not only with the Sovereign's state but also with the thought of a Maori kingdom. By 1858 the first Maori king had been elected, mostly by the Maoris of the centre and north of the North Island. The old man chosen, Te Wherowhero, ruled with much protocol under the title of 'Potatau the First'. His court was divided among itself: there were the moderates, who felt that the Maori could well afford to be friendly to the pakeha so long as no more land was sold, and there were the extremists who wished to push every white man into the sea. The King movement could never be said to be effective, especially as many of the tribes refused to acknowledge the Maori king at all, but it did provide a forum where land problems could be thoroughly discussed. Thus Wiremu Kingi was not a supporter of the King movement but he did agree with the moderate Kingite ideas on the land issue.

The King movement and all it represented constituted only a mild and natural reaction to the attitude of the average European settler. The Maoris had believed the missionaries, had believed in the Waitangi agreement and had trusted in Grey, but the main body of pioneers, although enterprising, were not washed in the milky waters of humanitarianism. Mostly they disliked the apparently lazy, brown-skinned people who maintained a firm grip on the land for which they had come so far. To the ordinary white man the Maori seemed a frightening and unpleasant person, obviously inferior in every way, and he took no trouble to conceal his antagonism. So the Maori Wars were also a series of race conflicts, as well as a struggle for the land. In 1861 Grey was recalled for his second term as Governor. He saw his job mostly as cleaning up the mess left by Gore Browne and he tried to introduce a system of justice to protect the Maoris, but he was too late because those who desired this were already Kingites. When he realised the strength of the King movement and the failure of his measures, he became convinced that the capital was in danger and persuaded the British Government to send troops to defend it. War finally broke out in 1863 with all the truculence and suspicion of the King movement behind the Maori fighting force. Unlike the course of the war in Taranaki, this was a series of military campaigns which the Maoris were bound to lose eventually, although their courage and military strategy performed amazing feats.

During the conflict some terrible seeds were sown, one straggling plant appearing almost before the main war had come to an end. The British troops burnt all Maori settlements in their path and one warrior saw his two daughters die in this way. As an instrument of revenge he took up a new religion called Pai Marire which quickly gained many supporters, especially in the isolated east coast areas. These Maoris maintained bursts of sporadic fighting until long after the official peace, keeping the whole of the North Island in a state of constant alarm. The new religionists were called Hau Haus — from the sound of the Amen to their chants — and combined a peculiar mixture of their cast-off Christianity and their own old paganism. In the name of Pai Marire (literally 'good and peaceful'), many atrocities were committed right across the island. Indeed, the small, struggling settlement of Wanganui was only saved from extinction by the heroic battle fought against the Hau Haus on its behalf by the friendly local Maoris. When the Government forces tried to pursue the perpetrators of these outrages the Hau Haus retired quickly into the deep bush fastnesses where it was quite impossible to follow. This sort of fighting kept up until 1867 and was beginning to die away when in the following year a new disturbance in the form of Te Kooti Rikirangi put further terror into the settlers' hearts. Te Kooti had perhaps unjustly been exiled to the Chatham Islands from which he finally escaped, breathing vengeance on all white men. He was a military genius in his own right and was never captured. The friendly Maoris fighting for the Crown won their full share of glory following his movements across the back country. Te Kooti remained a danger until it became clear that the angry but defeated Kingites would not have him for their leader. He finally retired to the centre of the North Island where he reorganised the new religious faith of Ringatu — another combination of paganism and Christianity. The Ringatu religion has adherents today and is certainly Te Kooti's most lasting contribution to New Zealand history.

The causes of the Maori Wars reveal the white man in a very discreditable light. The empire building of Donald McLean together with the inability of a weak Governor to withstand the pressure of greedy settlers led to a reversal of hitherto firmly held land policies. The part played by the Maori himself was a natural one in the circumstances; he was afraid for his land and ultimately for himself. He had reason to fear, just as the settlers had reason for extending the frontier. It seems fairly clear that sooner or later a conflict was inevitable as it has been in every other country where similar problems existed. The results of the Maori Wars on the other hand were not as inevitable as the conflict. The Government faced with an acute shortage of money to pay for the war, aggravated by provincial rivalry, pursued a rigorous policy whereby the rebellious Maoris lost their land by confiscation. The land was to be sold to the settlers in order to pay off the war debt and open up the North Island to the development postponed by the war.

Three large blocks of land were impounded but before they could be profitably split up by the speculators the Government had an inconvenient commitment to settle. The Colonial Office insisted that all loyal Maoris who had lost land by the confiscation should be recompensed; but because of the principle of tribal land-holding, it was very difficult to distinguish which land belonged to this loyal Maori or that rebel one. In the end, the profits from the confiscated land vanished as sizeable areas were returned to the Maoris and yet further money had to be paid out for development and resettlement of the land that was retained. But, if the profit vanished into thin air, the bitter taste left by the conflict remained. It was now legal to buy land directly from Maoris and a Native Land Court was established to make sure of the validity of a seller's rights to the land – the principle of joint or tribal negotiation had gone by the board. It is ironical that the Land Court inquiry into the details of the Waitara confiscation found the position of Wiremu Kingi to be even stronger than he himself had claimed. However, any Maori with a valid claim could now sell tribal land if he wished, and many did. From this time onward Maori land was sold very quickly and by 1900 little good land remained in Maori hands.

It is difficult to make any general statement about the attitude of the white people towards the Maoris once the battles and the skirmishes were over. Some pakehas held a benignly pessimistic view – the inroads of European diseases had taken a much greater toll of the Maori population than the disasters of the wars, and the birth rate was declining rapidly. These humanitarians were pleased to assist the Maori race to a comfortable and not unpleasant demise. On the other hand, many settlers undoubtedly felt rage and hostility against the Maori people who in defence of their own heritage were standing in the way of the promised land that was to be. The Maoris, whose fierce dignity and pride had received such terrible insults at the hands of their Christian compatriots, made no secret of their feelings. They withdrew into the shell of their own culture, lacking, it appeared, even the will to survive as a race.

These heavy troubles belaboured the North Island for a long ten years, a time of great progress in the South Island. Large sheep stations were claimed and explored along the foothill ranges of the Southern Alps and across the tussock plains to the sea. South Island colonies thrived and grew wealthy on the wave of wool and rectitude which organised their roads and refused financial assistance to the stricken north to help pay for the wars. Christchurch, the City of the Plains, deliberately increased its English Anglican atmosphere, while Dunedin, the Scottish southern city, was infused with an appropriately dour prosperity. In fact, these two Provinces, so far ahead of the others in settlement and development, were jealous rivals at a time when it was still a case of each Province for itself. This pragmatic rivalry underlined the realities of existence. The two islands were separated by a stretch of stormy water but the Central Government, transferred from Auckland to Wellington in 1865, was a convenient reminder that New Zealand was still one colony even though the more affluent members of it could not bring themselves to help their less fortunate fellows in another province.

In 1861, while the province of Taranaki was besieged with warfare, Gabriel Reid, one of the ever-hopeful itinerant prospectors of the South Island, discovered gold at Tuapeka, near Dunedin. Almost overnight the province of Otago was overwhelmed with a gold rush, as people poured in from all over New Zealand, from Australia and even further off to make their fortune. Such merchants of Dunedin as could resist the fever made solid and lasting fortunes by staying at home and supplying the miners with flour, picks and shovels, and field transport. The necessities of life, swollen in value almost beyond price, trickled after the miners and their families as they explored and prospected much of Otago's inaccessible mountain country. Many of these people gave up the elusive quest and settled in the inhospitable valleys, seeking a more certain wealth on the sheep's back. The Gabriel's Gully strike put the newly established Bank of New Zealand on its feet. The Dunedin manager put out makeshift bank notes to tide the Bank over its first few weeks and immediately set up an assaying service which followed the miners over to the next great 'find' on the west coast of the South Island. Suddenly, in an almost uninhabited area, a population of 30,000 appeared. As in Otago, the merchants, the bankers and the land agents profited enormously and the country itself was tremendously enriched by the number of people who decided to settle and farm as well as by the gold exported.

It is easy to see now that the close of the Maori Wars with the great sell-out of Maori land, together with the gold rushes marked the beginning of the modern state of New Zealand. Both brought in their wake tremendous economic expansion which gave the colony as a whole a new vision of its possibilities and the confidence to reach out and seize the opportunity before it vanished. As always the land itself was the hard core of the dream with a quickly expanding pastoral development, but the gold rushes brought with them the people to work the dream — an urban labouring class prepared to do almost anything for a living — which changed for good and all the founding colonists' ideals of a genteel eighteenth-century society in the South Seas.

Chapter 4

Prosperity and Depression

THE PROSPERITY which accompanied the gold rushes was short-lived and the failure of confiscation policies to provide sufficient land at a reasonable price for the small purchaser led to widespread discontent. In the South Island more land was opened up but it remained a place for the expanding pastoralist, where the gold miner turned colonist was unwelcome except as hired labour. Unemployment became a problem first in the Otago province where a petition was presented to the Provincial Council demanding public work for the unfortunate men. Already the ordinary man looked to the Government to cure all ills, as his proper right and its duty. Indeed there was no other agency able to fill the role of benefactor and for local governments it was a case of needs must when the devil drives.

As conditions became steadily worse a young Jewish journalist named Julius Vogel emerged as a considerable figure in the Central Government. Although originally an ardent provincialist representing Otago, he quickly saw that provincialism could only hold back the development so necessary to the country at this time. Grey's 1852 Constitution had established provincial government but had had nothing to say about secessions from the established provinces. At one stage Southland seceded but financial difficulties soon led to its re-absorption by Otago. Of the major provinces only two managed their affairs with sufficient skill to keep the price of land under control and maintain the development of social necessities. Otago and Canterbury had made considerable progress with road building and rail construction — Canterbury had built the world's longest rail tunnel through the Port Hills from Christchurch to Lyttelton, but even there social services lagged badly behind the need for them. By 1876 the Central Government had taken over not only the provincial debts but also the provincial functions of public works, railways and immigration.

With political adroitness of a high order Vogel espoused the

54

centralist cause, dropping his former friends without a backward glance. It suited his purposes much better to have the Central Government in full control; as Colonial Treasurer he put forward a scheme to borrow large sums of money against the credit of the whole colony to finance major public works to employ and keep employed the landless workers and to encourage further immigration. The poorer provinces having everything to gain and nothing to lose backed the new idea, really an old one writ large by a dynamic and forceful figure.

The greatest barrier to progress and development was poor communications. Vogel envisaged an enormous expansion of the existing services and the creation of new ones; only in this way could the country's trade flow more quickly. Vogel's policy of borrowing in all nearly twenty million pounds brought about all the results he had predicted. New roads were built, opening up large new areas of land and preparing the way for the large scale wheat farming which became a feature of the early 1880's. A steamship service was established to San Francisco, two steamship companies were founded and a cable was laid to Australia. Banks and other financial institutions as well as small secondary industries began to flourish. Unemployment vanished and immigration rapidly increased. Unfortunately the new immigrants were not very carefully selected and the old established colonists spurned the new arrivals who were mostly city dwellers and factory workers, wishing to continue their normal way of living but under better conditions. This wave of immigration saw the arrival of different nationalities attracted by the go-ahead economy – people from Scandinavia and Germany as well as from Britain.

In principle Vogel's idea was sound. A developing colony must mortgage future profits to pay for present expansion or it will never make any profit in the future. However, he was unfortunate in beginning his borrowing policy in the last three years of rising world prices before they began the slow but very steady fall which lasted until 1894. New Zealand had been caught up in the boom following the Franco-Prussian War which gave extra impetus to the amount of money coming into the country. Imports rose to an all-time peak in the Colony's history – the balance of payments problem had begun. Between 1870 and 1876, Vogel had had great difficulty in getting the provinces to recognise that consistent borrowing on a large scale required built-in safeguards. The provinces were too jealous of their land to allow him to set aside a proposed six million acres of the land opened up by public works as an endowment to repay the loans. The same men who refused to accept this sound provision refused also to allow forest conservation to be initiated. It was all too easy to plunge greedily on, completely swept away by the transformation taking place before their provincial eyes. Borrow, borrow, borrow more.

At this stage, in 1876, Vogel manœuvred the provinces out of existence as his administrative partners in the Government. He himself resigned and left for London as Agent-General for New Zealand, not a minute too soon. The drop in wool (the main export) prices had to some extent been concealed by the borrowing policy which had kept the economy buoyant, but financial crises in England and Australia caused many investors to withdraw their money. Once again the effect of this was masked, this time by the lending policy of the banks and other financial institutions, such as the expanding stock and station agents. The banks came on to the lending market largely as the result of a Privy Council decision that a bank could have a valid title to any land or property which it took as security for a loan. They were thus able to accommodate men wishing to farm the new tracts of land opened up by the public works; the banks and the stock and station agents lent enormous sums of money upon the security of the land itself. When the boom finally burst in 1879 New Zealand presented a picture of a country pulling itself up by its boot straps, always a difficult operation and one not usually successful. On the other hand, while the boom lasted the country received the injection of energy and capital it so urgently needed to make it a viable economic unit. New Zealand has been called a 'dependent economy' and the burst balloon in 1879 was the first indication that its very life depended on the outside world. However, it is a characteristic of dependent and developing economies that they need to borrow, and Vogel had produced the right answer both to overcome the setback of the sixties and to boost the country's development. He had the misfortune to borrow at the wrong time but it is doubtful whether there is ever a right time for a dependent economy to borrow. It is true that his policy improved communications but it saddled the country with a debt of staggering proportions, although had the Central Government and the provinces accepted his safeguards the load would have been at least bearable. In the event, however, it was not.

The warning lights had begun to blink much earlier than 1879 but the real state of affairs was disguised by the flow of bank credit so that the withdrawal of overseas capital was hardly noticed at the time. The growing seriousness of the situation was most clearly revealed by the steady drop in wool prices which eventually affected everyone in the Colony. Wheat prices also fell and the early 1880's saw a temporary recession become a full-scale depression which was to drag on until the late 1890's. Wool prices continued to fall; people emigrated to Australia where they thought things could not be as bad, and landowners were left with enormous mortgages which they had raised to increase the size of their holdings. As the main banking institution of the Colony, the Bank of New Zealand had the doubtful privilege of owning much of the farming land of New Zealand.

Once the ebullient excitement of the Vogel policy subsided the Government of the day did its best to cope with an unpleasant and rapidly worsening situation. The changes which took place as a result of the long and near-disastrous economic crisis remain today, germane to the development of the country and to the formation of its political doctrines. At the time, in the late 1870's, there were, by and large, few political loyalties to separate the members of Parliament into anything like a party system. Apart from the central core forming the administration, the House of Representatives formed and re-formed itself around the issues of the day somewhat in the manner of an intricate dance.

The continuous Conservative Ministry which ruled the country throughout most of the period was more than a little handicapped by its very nature. These representatives of the people were the gentlemen of the Colony, educated men with professional standing, or backed by the status of large estates. They were not ready to hear the growing and vociferous demands of the small man who asked for a reasonable freehold upon which to employ himself. Although their own large estates were usually heavily mortgaged, landowners were reluctant to share the source of the country's potential wealth. Times would surely improve and the goldmine would come into its own again. However, as a result of the lack of any sort of strict party philosophy or alignment, there were several forward-looking and notably radical men in the Government, who put up measures as liberal as any which the growing left-wing coterie had to offer. Harry Atkinson, the Prime Minister, attempted unsuccessfully to get the idea of a universal pension scheme accepted by the House; he foresaw growing urban distress and tried to remove some of it before it increased too much. Also, William Rolleston espoused the radical cause of a leasehold rental which would have given the little man what amounted to a perpetual leasehold of Crown lands. Predictably, the Conservative majority in the House of Representatives could not bring itself to pass such measures, nor could it dissociate itself from the sense of personal threat that was inherent in legislation of this nature.

Not only was the Conservative Ministry constitutionally incapable of reforming the land policy of the Colony, but it was also, in spite of Atkinson's lead, at a loss to deal with the growing distress and unrest in the towns. Many of the urban workers had come for the gold and stayed for the profits of the boom time; indeed, some had been enticed to immigrate by the promise of these same profits, but now many were hungry and more were unemployed. The small secondary industries which were surviving the depression forced their workers to accept low wages and poor conditions. This was especially so in the clothing industry, where a horrified observer noted from his pulpit that workers in New Zealand were being exploited in just the way they had travelled thousands of miles to escape. An active, though largely unco-ordinated trade union movement was the natural result of this sort of unrest, and it readily joined hands with the growing number of men who could see only a radical answer to the problems of the time.

This small band of men – mostly gentlemen with modified socialist leanings – had allied themselves under Sir George Grey's banner when he came out of retirement to defend the provinces he had created in the 1852 Constitution. As a force in Parliament he never counted for much (not even in his brief spell as Prime Minister), but he promulgated the most liberal doctrine the country had yet heard. Between 1877 and 1887 Liberals as such were elected to the House of Representatives, often with the support of the infant trade union organisations. Liberal reform measures were introduced by these independent members but always refused by the legislature. Then, under the pressure of an economy becoming more and more distressed, the Liberal men in the House united, and in 1889 the new political party was born, with John Ballance as its leader. The party's strength quickly increased; its position was enhanced by the fact that it had something to offer to the ordinary unlanded people, whereas the Conservatives went to the hustings with a tighten-your-belt-boys-there's-worse-to-come policy.

In 1890 the Liberal Party came into power. Once in office it set out immediately to relieve, not so much the distressed economy, as the desperate people within the economy. If the party was largely infused with the flavour of socialism, it was not a communistic socialism, but rather one in which the people were regarded as the State. The State was therefore bound to do everything in its power to assist its members in every way—literally from the cradle to the grave. The Liberal Cabinet contained men anxious to put into practice different aspects of this creed—from John McKenzie with his land policies to William Pember Reeves the intellectual—and it says much for Ballance that he was able to give the party a coherent and steady leadership in those first heady and difficult years of power. A man who has often been underestimated, mostly because of the short two years of his premiership, Ballance held the respect of the very different elements in his Cabinet without losing sight for an instant of what the party was trying to do. It was he who pushed the first of McKenzie's land schemes through the House of Representatives, and when they were repeatedly 'frozen out' of the Legislative Council, forced the incoming Governor to appoint more liberal members to that body.

Ballance was on very strong ground for the Liberals had won their election on a policy of land reform. Once again, New Zealand was in the midst of a reappraisal, and as always, it concerned the people and the land. The population had risen considerably and more people wanted a share of the land, most of which by this time was held privately or by the Crown. Until the successful experiment with refrigerated meat in 1882, the only exportable commodity New Zealand produced in any quantity was wool and wool growing on a large scale called for big runs. The voyage of the *Dunedin*, carrying a refrigerated cargo from Port Chalmers to London, opened a new and a wider horizon. Not only meat but dairy products could be refrigerated, and the dairy farms could be small farms, owned and worked by one man and his family.

John McKenzie had come to New Zealand from Scotland and he was determined to prevent in his new country the evils of exclusive landlordism which he had left behind in the old. He and his party concentrated on settling more people on farms, either directly under a lease-in-perpetuity on Crown land or indirectly, by imposing a graduated land tax penalising large holdings which helped force land out of private ownership. Generally speaking, the Liberals considered land too much of a public asset to be allowed to pass permanently into private hands. McKenzie and later Seddon between them also arranged State finance to help small farmers.

The egalitarianism of the New Zealander was very much present in these measures, though in their concept of leasehold 'ownership' the Liberals, perhaps more than a little blinded by the theories of Bentham and Mill, failed to appreciate sufficiently the individualistic character of the New Zealand farmer. As long as he could not afford his own freehold, the small farmer was pleased to accept a leasehold, but early in the next century, when the depression had given way to better times, dairy farmers were strong in their demand to purchase their farms. This is an interesting sidelight upon the New Zealand character, which often expresses itself in a determination to have one's cake and eat it too. From the beginning, social legislation of an apparently extreme kind has gone hand in hand with a demand for capitalistic independence. In any case, this explains the failure of the Liberals to introduce 'land nationalisation' or even to maintain completely the Crown freehold.

Land reform was the demand of the country, and the Liberals effected it, and continued to do so after the death of Ballance and well into the reign of the new leader, Richard John Seddon. King Dick, as he was popularly known, was a large, dominating man with a flair for tactical politics and a shrewdness that kept his party safely in power through vicissitudes which would have toppled a lesser man. More than this, his bluff front served as a good protection for the policies of his thinner-skinned colleagues; behind it, Reeves was able to put into practice sweeping labour experiments the like of which the world had dreamt about but never seen.

Reeves himself was a New Zealand-born intellectual gentleman, one of the first the country had produced, in a Cabinet where most of the Ministers were not well educated. He bore a perpetual chip on his shoulder and carried with him a sense of failure which contrasted oddly with the evangelical zeal he brought to the mission of 'socialising' labour conditions in New Zealand. He had read deeply among European theorists on labour and the management of capital, and adapted what he found there to local conditions. Already in New Zealand he found a country which had accepted in principle the idea that it was the Government's responsibility earnestly to promote social welfare, if only negatively, by protecting the people from the worst blows of fortune. Reeves was especially interested in the State's protective role. He had watched an abortive strike and had seen how little, if anything, the strikers had gained, and what a great deal they and their families had lost. Accordingly he promoted the Industrial Conciliation and Arbitration Act, which provided a special Court to preside over compulsory conciliation discussions between employers and workers, in the hope of fending off strikes before they became inevitable. The effect of this Act has been enormous and the Court of Arbitration has grown into a body which not only keeps industrial contenders at a distance but also makes wage orders affecting the whole community. This Act, which aroused little general interest at the time, was Reeves' own invention. He had read and meditated upon untried theories and from them framed a working system of labour relations far in advance of anything in existence at that time.

Along with the Industrial Conciliation and Arbitration Act, Reeves brought into being a complex of labour laws and regulations which set the pattern for industrial conditions for many years — one or two of the provisions were so far ahead of their time that they have scarcely needed revision. Among various other employment provisions, he regulated working hours and conditions in factories, fixed a minimum age for workers and provided time off for them during working hours. New Zealand was the first country in the world to give its shop assistants either chairs or lunch hours. To supervise the implementation of this legislation Reeves formed and administered a Labour Department which provided inspectors to look into every branch of employment in the country. The odd thing about Reeves' enactments was that there was almost no pressure for them. They were his ideas on how labour relations should be governed and he was lucky to have a Liberal administration to try them out. At a time when the burning issue was the land question, Reeves' legislation went into force quietly — noticed more by socialists overseas than by the people at home.

The Liberal Government of the 1890's, like the Labour Government of the 1930's, is often credited with breaking the depression. It is true that its policies helped but the seeds of economic recovery had been sown even before it took office. The invention of refrigeration did much to help the stricken economy by diversifying production and exports, and the closer settlement encouraged by the Liberals promoted more intensive land use and therefore higher productivity. Also in the mid-nineties, world prices began a slow recovery and by the end of the century the country was back on solid ground and beginning to advance.

The Liberals remained in power until 1912 when they were unseated by growing social forces which they were unwilling to recognise or accommodate. After the death of Ballance the party was led by Seddon and later by Joseph Ward. McKenzie retired, worn out, in 1899 and the wasp-like Reeves was sent off to London as Agent-General for New Zealand in 1896. From then on Seddon ran a one-man band. Born in Lancashire, he emigrated to Australia and thence to the west coast goldfields where he identified himself completely with the miners and their hardships. He kept his identification with the common people so that he always remained 'one of us'; indeed he knew a phenomenal number of them personally. It was the secret of his electoral success and it remained with him until he died in 1908. As he grew more sure of his political footing, his policies were dictated not so much by what the people wanted (though in fact he never moved far away from the wishes of the ordinary man) as by his own conscious desire to serve them. This was the motive for his most important social legislation – the introduction of the old age pension. He described himself as a humanitarian, and this word perhaps defines the spirit of New Zealand's brand of socialism better than any other. In the name of humanity alone a government must provide opportunity for everyone to enjoy the good things of life and to use its full resources to care for the poor, the aged and the downtrodden. In any case this was Seddon's view of himself and of his mission as Prime Minister and he so believed it that the rest of New Zealand believed it also. Both the country and its Prime Minister had such faith in this ebullient father-figure that he could do anything. Another government could well have been brought down by the personal financial indiscretions of Ward, the Treasurer, during the 1895 financial crises, when the State stepped in to save the Bank of New Zealand and, incidentally, to become a major shareholder. Another Prime Minister might well have become uneasy about his opponents' criticisms of political patronage in making important appointments, but not Seddon. He was enormous, well-wishing, often uncouth, with a tremendous vitality; the country was very content to warm itself in the climate of his geniality. There were

dissident voices of course but while Seddon lived they remained crying to themselves in the wilderness.

On Seddon's death Joseph Ward was left to maintain an increasingly uneasy administration until 1912, when the long reign of the
Liberals came to an end. Even while Seddon was alive there were
factions within the party, but King Dick's political dominance had
managed to contain them. The troubles were a phenomenon of the
country's social development. The Liberals, largely aided by rising
world prices, had given a progressive if humdrum stability to the
economic structure, but slowly different sections of the community
began to make further demands upon the Government. Times had
been particularly good to the small dairy farmers of the North
Island; these were the people who had been established by the early
policies of the Liberal Government and continued to be handsomely
accommodated by this administration, especially by way of State
credit. They formed one section of opinion — the right wing. Unfortunately, the country's prosperity had not effectively seeped through
to the working man whose pay packet had remained much the same
for a decade, in spite of appreciable industrial expansion. The representatives of these people made up the second section of the party —
the left wing.

It was generally agreed that the farmers were 'the backbone of
the country' and therefore entitled to the lion's share of the benefits.
However, the small farmer with a lease wanted to purchase his freehold for the very good reason that he could not use leasehold land as
security for the credit offered by the Government, nor could he take
advantage of the rising land prices to join in the general property
exchange which was such a feature of the post-depression years. The
small farmer wanted the right to his freehold — but at its original
unimproved value! The new political party which espoused this
cause was called the Reform Party, a small right-wing breakaway
from the Liberals. It slowly drew more and more conservative support, under its leader William Ferguson Massey, as it took over the
hitherto hopeless role of Opposition to the Government. Reform
Party strength increased steadily as the socialistic menace of the
Liberal left wing grew more pronounced.

Joseph Ward was caught in a cleft stick. He could not move fast
enough towards the farmers to prevent the growth of the Reform
Party, and whatever moves he did make towards purchase of leasehold only succeeded in further alienating his disaffected Labour

supporters. Different splinter groups were formed, mostly infused with the spirit of nineteenth-century socialism, but the most concrete measure of the growth and coherence of the Labour movement was the election of two independent Labour members to Parliament in 1911. Ward had done well to hold on for so long after Seddon's death; indeed, although Massey emerged in 1912 as the new Prime Minister, the parties were so equal that a tough and unyielding term of office lay before him. He immediately kept his platform promises about the purchase of leasehold land at its original price, after which only a very small proportion of leaseholders chose to take advantage of the legislation. The principle had been a rallying cry around which to focus an ill-defined but very real dissatisfaction with the Liberal Government – a disenchantment based on the farmers' fear not only of socialism but also of industrial labour as a class.

There was much unrest among the Trade Unions. The Arbitration Court had so frozen wages that while the cost of living had gone up, the worker's pay had not. Another major grievance lay in the arbitration system itself which was designed to prevent strikes not only by the principle of compulsory conciliation but also by encouraging small unions to negotiate for themselves, thus drawing the teeth of a united Labour movement. However, in 1909 a Federation of Labour was formed, binding together many unions in a loosely knit syndicate capable of negotiating and striking, if necessary, on behalf of all members. The issue came violently into the open in 1912 when goldminers at Waihi went on strike. The miners had used the Federation of Labour to obtain a wage increase, at the same time exercising their right to withdraw from the arbitration system. The employers found a loophole in the Act, registered a small number of their men as a goldminers' union and negotiated a new award which then became binding on all workers in the mining industry. Not unnaturally, the miners struck, but a somewhat nasty partnership between employers and a farmers' Government was not going to allow industrial unrest, especially at a time when conditions were becoming tighter. A band of strike-breakers was hired by the mine owners and escorted into Waihi by the police; there was considerable confusion and not a little violence, during which one of the strikers was killed and the leaders finally imprisoned.

In 1913 the splinters of Labour came together in a United Federation of Labour and a political party, the Social Democrats, was formed. The leaders of the Federation, men who were later to lead the first Labour Government, were inclined to extreme measures but the members of the Social Democratic Party were more moderate — their remedy for the working man's problem lay in Parliament. Unfortunately for both these bodies, the year of their birth proved also to be the year of their death. A Wellington dock dispute again brought out the unholy alliance of employers, Government and farmers and the strike was broken, quickly and brutally. Massey was generally considered to have vindicated himself as leader of a party openly acknowledging its vested interests. At the same time, it is impossible to overlook the savage bitterness of this snatch of class warfare. In 1916 the New Zealand Labour Party emerged.

In spite of these troubles New Zealand was still a comfortable, humdrum, prosperous country, and it remained so even through the years of the Great War. Massey and Ward joined in a wartime coalition and New Zealand supported the British cause with patriotic ardour, a large number of fighting men and a great deal of agricultural produce. Seddon had involved New Zealand in its first war on Britain's behalf, the Boer War, mostly because he was an imperialist at heart, but it is safe to say that popular sentiment towards the 'home' country enabled the Government to give far greater support in 1914 than Britain could ever have expected. Certainly, it was not all the doing of Massey, himself a notoriously lukewarm Commonwealth man. New Zealand and Australian troops took part in the ill-conceived campaign in the Dardanelles and their gallantry against the Turks has become a by-word in the story of heroism. After the ANZAC disaster, New Zealanders fought in the bitter European trench war until the end of hostilities.

The Maori people also joined in the cause, contributing a complete unit, the 'Maori Battalion'. Famous as fighters, the existence of the battalion stood for something more important than a desire to support Britain in a European war. After their defeat in the 1860's and the confiscation of their lands, the Maori people fell into a decline. The tribes wrapped themselves in a cloak of isolation which they did not begin to discard until a decade after the end of the wars. Slowly, however, they emerged, if only to acquire the goods possessed by the pakeha. Some Maoris became farm labourers, others tried to farm their lands along the profitable pakeha lines, while still more sold and leased land for European settlement. This kind of activity suggested that the Maori, if not actually forthcoming, was

at least reconciled to the fact of permanent European settlement.
Yet, in a curious way, this was belied by the Maoris' apparent lack
of will to survive as a race; the birth rate dropped alarmingly and it
appeared in 1896 as if the Maori people were likely to die out. Not
only did the birth rate decrease, but a high mortality rate made great
inroads in the population. The Maoris were still very vulnerable to
European diseases such as tuberculosis, scarlet fever and measles—
the diseases with which their traditional remedies could not cope.
They had come down from their hillside pas, where the old sanita-
tion methods had been effective, if somewhat crude, and were now
mostly living on lowland flats or even over swamps. Traditional
hygiene had been forgotten, resulting in general ill-health. In 1896
the number of Maoris was forty thousand, only a fraction of the
population in 1840.

Furthermore, chiefly authority declined as the Land Courts super-
vised more and more closely the sale of Maori lands. Individualistic
legislation reduced the legal status of the chief to that of an individual member of the tribe—doubtless a democratic thought, but not
the way Maori society went about its business. Their leaders having
lost their mana, the tribes began to disintegrate, missing the stabilising focus of the traditional pattern. Without leaders, the race lost
much of its initiative, in spite of the fact that Maoris were represented in Parliament from 1867. However, the Maoris are a remarkable people, and from within came a slow recovery of morale and a
willingness to live with and benefit by European standards and skills.
The birth rate began to rise (until today Maoris number a thirteenth
of the total population). At the same time, new leaders emerged who
were able to stand for the Maori in the pakeha community without
alienating themselves from their own people. Educated in European
schools and universities, these men were all connected, for a time at
least, with the Young Maori Party, a semi-political organisation
which did much to revive the Maori's pride in his race and culture.
Sir Peter Buck, who later became one of the world's leading Polynesian anthropologists, and Sir Maui Pomare were both able to
make a tremendous contribution to the problems of Maori health,
helping to break down Maori resistance to European medicine. Sir
James Carroll (at one time Acting Prime Minister) and later Sir
Apirana Ngata both urged better Maori land policies upon the House
of Representatives, and throughout his long term in Parliament (he
died in 1950) Ngata worked ceaselessly among his own people to

improve standards of farming on the land that remained to them. These leaders were outstanding men in any company; they emerged at the end of the nineteenth century and worked on well into the twentieth, combining in themselves the very best of European and Maori culture. It is interesting that each of these men was part-Maori, part-pakeha; perhaps a significant signpost towards the future. In any case, they helped revive the Maoris' pride in their national inheritance and customs (Maoritanga), and brought themselves to the notice of the pakeha population, not as an inconvenience which was happily dying out, but as a living race which would play an important part in the future development of the country.

The end of the First World War brought Massey his first and only satisfactory electoral victory. Always he had struggled on with a small, unhappy majority — the Labour vote was growing and there were still many Liberals who did not relish government by a small farmers' party. However, Joseph Ward had opted out of the wartime coalition just before the end of hostilities, and Massey received solitary credit for the victory. Once more, he had an unpleasant row to hoe. During the war, New Zealand had enjoyed a quietly virtuous boom and the country had grown to rely on high prices for farming products in England's captive wartime market. The marketing was done in bulk — in effect, Britain 'commandeered' agricultural produce for the duration of the war. Private competition was thus eliminated and a Board of Trade, assisted by the State whenever necessary, regulated the internal economy of New Zealand. Prices remained high for two years after the war, then fell as the British contracts ran out. As always, farmers looked to the Government for help; the result was the establishment of a Meat Board and then a Dairy Board. These Boards were mostly composed of producers' representatives, but there was also some Government representation. With the return of competitive marketing, the task of the Boards was to control marketing generally, so that a flood of produce would not arrive on the British market to drive the price down. The Meat Board was largely successful, but the Dairy Board aimed too high and so mismanaged its affairs that one season's production was 'boycotted' by the British buyers. Massey was attacked by Labour because the Boards were not entirely in the hands of the State, but to the urban business wing of his party the whole arrangement smacked altogether too much of tampering with the course of trade.

Massey was also in trouble over a land bubble which burst very quickly with the fall in prices. The Government had settled returned servicemen on farms or else had given them credit to purchase on their own account. Land prices rocketed and farms changed hands very frequently at inflated prices, and there were many evils attendant on the speculation. Experienced farmers sold out to ex-servicemen many of whom had never farmed before; some farmers were settled on hopelessly unsuitable land which even in the best of times would not have yielded a living. Had overseas prices held up, the trouble might have slowly worked itself out of the system, but credit fluctuated violently and many farmers were caught with large mortgages and high interest bills. Overseas prices fluctuated distressingly. The years from 1921 to 1924 saw a down swing, followed by a recovery in 1925 and 1926, another drop and recovery in 1928 and then the long, long fall as the whole world fell into the trough of the Great Depression. New Zealand's economy was heavily dependent on overseas markets and faithfully reflected every tremor, every hesitancy of the world's finances. The farmers became not so much fearful as puzzled and frustrated; it was not enough for a farmer to work hard and farm well to get a reasonable return from his land. It is not surprising that throughout this period the farming vote wavered in its loyalty to Reform, seeking wherever it could some answer to price fluctuations beyond apparent control.

The Reform Party was the instrument of the small farmer, just as its leader seems the epitome of the people he represented. Massey was a solid man of dogged virtue and limited vision. He believed in private enterprise and the freehold; he believed that the farmer was his own best financial adviser, especially where marketing was concerned. Beyond this he did not go, except to maintain his party in power by sheer force of determination and the country quota – a quaint arrangement whereby the rural population was given electoral parity with urban dwellers by counting in 28 per cent of imaginary voters. In practice, the Liberal Party often supported the Government against the Labour representatives, but at election time Liberal and Reform competed for votes. The growing strength of Labour in the towns suggested the amalgamation of the two farmers' parties, but Ward and Massey were so out of sympathy that this occurred only when both were dead.

Massey died in 1926 and Gordon Coates won Reform's best election victory in 1925. He was Prime Minister until 1928, when

the country, in search of an answer to the economic conundrum, tried
the Liberal solution. Coates was a man of different outlook from
Massey; he was younger and a second-generation New Zealander,
accustomed to the idea of turning the machinery of Government to
economic purposes. He was also ready to listen to advice. It was
unfortunate for him that the temporary recovery of 1925 did not
last until the next election, when the electors succumbed to Sir
Joseph Ward's dream of a financial cornucopia. The now ancient
Liberal leader promised to borrow an enormous sum which would
restore New Zealand's prosperity and pay everyone's debts. In fact,
the party intended to borrow £7,000,000, but an error magnified
the amount to £70,000,000. The Liberals swept the country and the
unfortunate Ward spent a harassed eighteen months in office before
he died.

His successor was George Forbes, a sincere and honest farmer
without the ability to cope with a disastrous depression. In 1930,
however, he was at least sufficiently discerning to realise that the
depression had arrived and that optimism was an unrealistic policy.
The two farmers' parties at last united and won the 1931 election
with a mandate to deal with conditions as they were. Forbes remained Prime Minister with Coates as his deputy. By 1931 the
whole economy was a reflection of the farmers' problem. In
three years the national income dropped from £150,000,000 to
£90,000,000. The typical farmer's receipts dropped by nearly 40 per
cent, but with heavy mortgage commitments his outgoings remained
almost the same. Business suffered as the farmer spent less, wages
fell and by 1933 there were 80,000 people unemployed and hungry.
In some cities angry, frustrated people rioted in the streets, more a
demonstration of impotence and despair than of revolutionary
feeling.

The United Party tried hard, but its Finance Minister, William
Downie Stewart, was too conservative to see beyond economising at
home and increasing exports. Stewart was still tied to the idea of a
balanced budget, by 1933 an economic as well as a practical anachronism. He resigned in this year, however, on the question of devaluation which offended one of the main principles in his economic
credo. An unsuccessful Finance Minister, he is still of interest in
being the last Cabinet Minister in New Zealand to resign on a
matter of principle, perhaps a commentary on modern New Zealand
society. He was replaced as Finance Minister by Coates who at once

began to carry out the advice of a special group of economic experts. In the face of considerable conservative opposition he increased the exchange rate more sharply than the banks had done in 1931: £100 sterling was now equal to £125 N.Z. He established the Reserve Bank of New Zealand partly to obtain cheaper credit for Government borrowing but mainly to secure more control over general monetary policy. To ease the farmers' load he reduced mortgage interest rates and set up a National Mortgage Corporation to help supply cheap credit. Slowly these measures had their effect, helped a great deal by a small but steady rise in overseas prices.

Apparently Coates had worked the miracle. It was his great misfortune that this sort of work needs to be viewed from a distance. People in work camps, living on the smell of Government relief, teachers, surveyors, architects, tradesmen, unemployed or barely employed, could not feel the shuddering economy stagger to its feet. Farmers lent a ready ear to easy-money political theorists and the Labour Party continued its trenchant criticism of the Government. By 1935, the country was ready to hear the Labour proposals. It had taken almost exactly three decades for the Labour Party to learn the lesson of socialism in New Zealand: to get into power, Labour needed a big farming vote. It had to overcome the farmers' suspicion that it was an anarchist left-wing organisation which would nationalise the means of production, distribution and exchange. The party learnt well; it dropped its ultra-socialist tendencies and transformed itself into a fast moving political group espousing socialist humanitarianism. In fact, it was the newly-emergent Liberal Party of 1901 all over again, although faced with a different problem. In 1935, encouraged by the vigour of its attacks on the Government, small farmers and small businesses combined with industrial labour to sweep the Labour Party into power with an enormous majority under its leader Michael Joseph Savage.

Chapter 5

The Regulated State

THE NEW CABINET came brand-new to the business of administration, but it compensated with effort and zeal for its lack of experience. Some of the men had served time in Australian or New Zealand prisons for being industrial agitators or conscientious objectors; most were without formal education though one or two had read with a breadth and depth hardly characteristic of the twentieth century. The Finance Minister, Walter Nash, was probably the ablest man New Zealand has ever had in this position. He controlled the working of the whole economic system and was the main architect of the recovery legislation. The Minister of Health and Education was Peter Fraser, a fine administrator and a parliamentarian *par excellence*. He had a keen sense of political timing which, among other things, prevented him from claiming the party's leadership on the death of Harry Holland, that old Labour stalwart, who died shortly before the 1935 election. Fraser became Prime Minister on the death of Savage in 1940, to steer the country through years of war, prosperity and rising nationhood. He was perhaps the only statesman the country has ever had; his achievements become more apparent as the perspective of time reveals their true proportion.

Robert Semple was another member of the Cabinet with a flavour all his own. An accomplished soap-box orator, he is revered to this day for his heroic flow of epithet, condemnation and accusation, peppered with constructive thought – all without apparently drawing breath. The like of this oratory had not been heard in the House of Representatives since the Liberals, and it is doubtful if even then such a gift was to be found. Semple was Minister of Public Works. His great achievement was an immediate one; he opened up large-scale public works to employ men in labour camps and paid them a living wage. An even greater achievement, however, was to banish for ever the notion that men on road works could be used as beasts of burden. The age of machinery, Semple announced, had arrived in

71

New Zealand and while it took some years to implement the promise, the day of the wheelbarrow indeed departed. A less successful member of the victorious administration was John A. Lee, a left-wing socialist who was too influential to leave out of the executive, but who finally proved too great an embarrassment in it. An extremist, he appeared to his colleagues to demand the impossible too quickly and he was eventually expelled from the party in exceptionally bitter circumstances.

Another Minister of this Government to leave a lasting impression upon New Zealand was H. G. R. Mason, one of the few members of the Cabinet with a formal education of any consequence. A lawyer by profession, his clear, uncluttered mind was of immense value to his party. He was Attorney-General and Minister of Justice from 1935 to 1949 and again, in the next Labour Government, from 1957 to 1960. In his political career, he also held other portfolios, but it is as Attorney-General that he is largely remembered, mostly because of his unswerving determination to make the laws of New Zealand less contradictory and easier to interpret. His vocation has been a systematic examination of the law; his amendments mark the path of his achievement.

Savage, the new Prime Minister, himself possessed a personal charisma very like that of Seddon. He became leader of the Labour Party practically unknown to the general public, but began at once to present himself as the epitome of Labour's policies. Like Seddon, his great success lay in his ability to feel the public pulse, to project himself benevolently to any audience and receive a sympathetic response. His personal contribution to Labour's victory was great; the people needed to feel that government was reassuringly human and Savage's kindly father-image did much to play down some of Labour's more radical policies. As Prime Minister he grew considerably in stature, though his personal contribution to the development of the party's political theory was never great. He did not concern himself over-much with the details of his Departments, nor was he ever more than vague on questions of finance, but rather he set himself the task of public relations officer for his Government. In this role he was overwhelmingly successful; his smiling benevolence sold more social legislation than thousands of pamphlets on social justice. He was idolised by the country and died in 1940 still the most beloved leader New Zealand has ever had.

Once in power the party found itself in considerable need of the

Prime Minister's personal charm. Its electoral manifesto pledged the Government to provide for 'every person able and willing to work an income sufficient to provide him and his dependants with everything necessary to make a "home" and "home life" in the best meaning of those terms'. In 1936 the Government began to keep its promise. This was a year of hectic legislation, passed against a background of rising overseas prices. The Government bought out the private shareholders of the Reserve Bank and of the National Mortgage Corporation, which now became the State Advances Corporation. The theory of a State guarantee was invoked to cushion all sections of the community against further disastrous economic dislocation. For the farmer, this took the form of complete State control of marketing — the economy had been moving slowly towards this for many years. The farmer would sell his goods to the State which would pay him an average price taken over a number of years. In good years a reserve fund would accumulate to maintain the average price in bad years. In addition, the price to the farmer was to be a socially 'just' price, which would enable him to maintain a 'reasonable' standard of living. What is the definition of a 'just' price or exactly what constitutes a 'reasonable' standard of living has never been discovered; since the thirties New Zealand had not experienced times hard enough to clarify these issues. As it finally turned out, meat and wool continued to be sold competitively by producers or processers, but dairy farmers were only too pleased to accept the Government's plan.

If the farmers had their guarantee, so did the workers. Compulsory arbitration had been suspended by the United Party Coalition in an effort to prevent industrial unrest and unemployment, arbitration being a system that does not work well in a time of depression. The depression over, however, it became once more a protection for the worker, and the Labour Government restored it immediately along with a statutory minimum wage to give workers a more secure share of the country's income. The working week was reduced to forty hours for most workers and awards for overtime were made. In addition to regulations to increase the security of workers a controversial law was passed making trade union membership compulsory for all workers covered by an Arbitration Court award. The effect of this was enormous, not so much upon the individual worker as upon the Federation of Labour which was elevated into a powerful lobby in the Labour Party, able to threaten the stability of the whole economy by its wage order demands and strike potential. This very powerful body has not always been representative of its membership, because of a general apathy concerning all save the most controversial issues.

With the rise in overseas prices, farmers again began to spend, and the whole country felt the lift as more men were employed on farms and in business. The Government's public works policy helped, its State housing scheme employed men, its newly-active education system absorbed still more. However, though times were getting better, the moral of the last ten years was not forgotten – that while New Zealand remained dependent on overseas markets it would always be at the mercy of financial swings and trade recessions. The Government endeavoured to increase secondary industry as a means of diversifying the economy and reducing its dependence upon the land. In 1936 the Industrial Efficiency Act established a Bureau of Industry with comprehensive powers over secondary industries. At the time it frightened many producers who felt that it might be the thin end of the wedge of nationalisation of production, but the Act in practice did not live up to its title.

Finally, the Labour Government wished to provide a guarantee against the pitfalls of life itself. With the Social Security Act of 1938 New Zealand had the most comprehensive welfare system to be found anywhere in the world at that time. The legislation was unique in the range of the benefits it provided and for the sweeping powers of paternalism which it took to itself. The Act levied a special tax on all incomes to extend pensions, invalid benefits, and family allowances, and it instituted a national health service providing virtually free medical attention, drugs and maternity care. This Act was passed just before the next elections and it had the desired effect of diverting attention from the urgent balance of payments crisis waiting round the corner.

As might be expected, Labour won a resounding victory over the National Party, newly-risen from the ashes of the United Party and led by S. G. Holland. Labour then began to confront New Zealand's perennial problem of low overseas reserves and high consumption at home. Perhaps investors had taken fright at the thought of a socialist country – in any case, capital had flown and some large overseas loans fell due in the following year. Walter Nash found great difficulty in raising even short-term loans on the London money-market and import licensing was introduced to reduce imports. Fortunately for New Zealand's financial problems, however, the war broke out.

For the term of the war a special War Cabinet was set up and Fraser invited members of the Opposition to join it. Sidney Holland was reluctant to commit his party in this way, suggesting that a full-scale coalition between Labour and National should administer the country under wartime conditions. Labour rejected the suggestion and Holland, although he joined the Cabinet, resigned in 1942. Another member of the Opposition, however, took a prominent place in the Cabinet as Minister of Armed Forces and War Co-ordination. This was J. G. Coates, the former Prime Minister. Shabbily treated by the new National Party and elbowed out of its leadership, he found great scope for his undoubted administrative ability in the Cabinet, and his shrewd analysis of the problems of his portfolio won him the admiration and friendship of Peter Fraser, his erstwhile bitter enemy. This period was probably the crowning achievement of Coates' political life, because in it he was protected from the hurly-burly of the political rat race. Brilliant in his objective judgements outside the political field, his greatest weakness was an inability to sum up a politician on the make. He deserves more attention than he is commonly given, if only because he was the first Prime Minister of New Zealand to ask for and listen to the advice of experts; he was also the first Prime Minister of New Zealand to form a sound working relationship with his civil servants.

New Zealand had been alarmed at Japanese expansion and development earlier in the thirties and had taken steps to discover the extent of her protection against a Pacific enemy. The results of a series of talks with Britain and Australia were not particularly reassuring and Savage was about to institute compulsory military training to give New Zealand at least some internal defence, when the European situation worsened rapidly and Great Britain declared war on Germany. New Zealand immediately ranged itself alongside England, the first Commonwealth country to do so, entering a far-off European war from a strong sense of loyalty (where Britain stands, we stand) and also from a firm conviction of the justice of the cause.

The war years were formative ones for New Zealand in every way. On the home front the country committed itself to a total effort in producing food for Britain. Nash concentrated his economic policy around the idea of stabilisation. Britain provided an automatic outlet

for all New Zealand foodstuffs; the prices offered were not world
market prices but they were still good and the market was assured.
The greatest danger lay in internal inflation, with a great deal more
money in the hands of the people than there were goods to be purchased. This was countered by very heavy taxation and war loans,
and part of farmers' earnings was 'frozen' by the Government in
reserve funds. All essential commodities came under the jurisdiction
of a Price Tribunal which regulated retail prices, the general aim
being to 'peg' both wages and prices. The stabilisation policy was,
by and large, very successful; New Zealand ended the war with high
overseas reserves and with internal economic stability, but in achiev-
ing this the Government had gained substantial control over all
sections of the country's business. Much of this control was made
possible by the co-operation of the President of the Federation of
Labour, F. P. Walsh, whose command of the unions over this period
remained absolute and whose loyalty to Prime Minister Fraser was
never in doubt.

New Zealand's other wartime commitments proved more difficult
to manage. Considering the size of the country, a very large fighting
force was committed to the British war. The 1st Division embarked
for France, but before it arrived France had fallen. Instead, the men
went for their final training to Egypt, which itself became the scene
of a major front as the Germans penetrated the Mediterranean
and General Rommel spread into North Africa. Here, the New
Zealanders became a skilful mobile fighting unit under their commander, Bernard Freyberg. In his person as commander of an
independent Government's forces which were yet part of a wider
plan, Freyberg symbolised New Zealand's predicament. It was not
the first time New Zealand had contemplated the intricacies of
foreign affairs, but this time there could be no retreat into the fastnesses of the South Pacific. New Zealand had been a sovereign state
since 1907, with full control over its defence arrangements and its
involvement with other countries. In fact, its defence arrangements
had barely existed, thanks to the extensive might of British arms.
True, New Zealand had contributed food and men (the 1st Division)
to the First World War, but apart from a disastrous attempt to
govern Western Samoa under a League of Nations mandate, it had
taken little part either in Pacific politics or world affairs. Unlike
Vogel and Seddon, Massey had had an inward-looking policy. New
Zealand was a very lukewarm member of the League of Nations

and Massey saw little value in Commonwealth ties unless they were to be more definite than the Statute of Westminster finally set out. In the event, New Zealand did not ratify the Statute until 1947. Fraser, however, was a firm Commonwealth man, and his strong support of the idea of Commonwealth during and immediately after the war grew to a magnitude out of all keeping with the size of the country he represented. He insisted that the responsibility for New Zealand troops abroad lay finally upon their Government at home, otherwise the idea of independent co-operation meant nothing. If New Zealand troops were to disappear into the general array of forces under British command any idea of independent co-operation would be lost. Freyberg's commission was to take orders from the British commanders but in no way to commit New Zealand forces beyond the policy or approval of the Government. In an extremely difficult position Freyberg and Fraser worked remarkably well together, although relations became very strained at the time of the Greek campaign. Eventually, after largely assisting in the North African war, the 2nd Division moved with great distinction up through Italy and so to the end of the war in Europe.

Fraser's preoccupation with the Commonwealth ideal helped clarify the problem for the Government at the time of Pearl Harbor. The fall of the British naval base at Singapore very early in the Pacific war had cast great gloom upon the people of New Zealand. For the first time they considered the length of their coastline and the number of men already fighting in the Mediterranean. Even so, New Zealand was still a long way from Japan, but after Pearl Harbor and the Japanese drive south to the Solomons, New Zealand had every reason to feel naked and afraid. In a similar position, the Australian Government exercised its right to withdraw troops from the Middle East in order to defend its Pacific front. Strongly influenced by Fraser, the New Zealand Government rejected this course. With Churchill, the Prime Minister considered the symbolic value of the presence of Commonwealth troops alongside British forces in Europe to be of immense power — a final statement of the determination and the resources of the allied opposition to German domination. For all that, 1942 was spent by the country's leaders in frantically building up home defences; no further reinforcements were sent to the Middle East, home guard forces were reorganised and increased as much as possible and the 3rd Division in Fiji was built up to be a Pacific defence force. Relief came at last when the

American strength in the South Pacific could be increased to sizeable proportions and a division was sent to New Zealand to defend it if necessary. From this moment New Zealand, however reluctant, took its place as an actor in the drama of world affairs. It was increasingly unrealistic to expect defensive aid from Britain and however drawn by its social ties to pro-British attitudes, the fact remained, and has since grown abundantly clearer, that the United States must be New Zealand's most potent ally in the future, and this perhaps not merely for defensive considerations. At the time, however, the New Zealanders experienced a feeling of reprieve mingled with a less-than-gracious sentiment towards their rescuers, an attitude perhaps springing from a certain indignation that the country should have been placed in such a hazardous plight. At the same time, however, New Zealand saw that firm and active measures would be needed to prevent the Pacific (with New Zealand in it) being dominated by American interests. As a first step, Fraser insisted that New Zealand, as an allied power, should share garrison duties with the Americans in the Pacific and later in Japan, however much of a nuisance this small independent force might be. At the end of the war, New Zealand was at last ready to take its full place in the United Nations and to play a significantly independent part therein.

By 1943, New Zealand was beginning to experience an acute manpower shortage and a drop in food production seemed inevitable. The Government's answer was to rest some of the men who had been overseas for nearly four years. Almost 5,000 men were given a three months' furlough at home where their labour proved invaluable to the country. It had been decided to leave the 2nd Division in Europe until the end of the war and the furlough men were replaced at the expense of the 3rd Division in Fiji. Their furlough over, many of the men refused to return to the Middle East and they were supported by a population weary of war and very ready to leave the final blows for peace to be struck by someone else.

Thanks to the Government's financial policies during the war, the economy was in good shape to face the increasing complexities of a peacetime world. A Rehabilitation Department was set up to reestablish men in peacetime occupations without the economic dislocation which occurred after the First World War. Grants were made to returned servicemen for further education and for buying businesses, farms and houses. Prices rose and with the boom came overfull employment – a doubtful blessing indeed, with more jobs in the country than people to fill them. Inevitably, employers competed for labour and in spite of stabilisation, wages and prices rose. To the Labour Government the answer lay in higher taxation, increased subsidies on food and a further freezing of farmers' overseas incomes via appreciation of the exchange rate and stabilisation accounts. All sections of the community, however, demanded higher wages to keep up with the real earnings of the country; the Federation of Labour was constantly at the door of the Arbitration Court to obtain awards which set the economic standard for everyone. This complicated structure of economic controls had been slowly built up as the Government endeavoured to cushion New Zealand against the effects of economic fluctuations on world markets. The Government's failure to prevent internal inflation was roundly criticised by the 'private enterprise' National Opposition, under the vigorous leadership of Sidney Holland.

The period 1945–46 saw another outburst of welfare legislation again immediately before an election and perhaps to distract the voter's attention from the increasing number of inconvenient controls. Family allowances were increased to what was at the time a large sum of 10s. a week to be paid to the mother for every child in every family. Previously the benefit could be claimed only by poor families on the birth of the second and subsequent children. In one year the cost to the State rose from £2,000,000 to £12,000,000, a leap which cannot be adequately justified even under the heading of social humanitarianism. However, it did seem right and proper that family men should receive greater tax deductions and that the health scheme should be broadened. The Bank of New Zealand was also nationalised completely, after half a century's operation under the Government's wing. This was a logical step, but it aroused considerable discussion in a community impatient at frequently inefficient, always ponderous, departmental administration of Government controls.

The welfare legislation was not, however, sufficient to allay the country's discontent with the Labour administration. As it was, the 1946 election split the pakeha vote equally between the two parties, and Labour was only returned to power by a majority of four, given by the loyalty of the Maori electorates. From the very first the Labour Party had not only made great promises to the Maoris, but had gone out of its way to keep them. For the first time, a European government realised that it was not enough to make available to the

Maoris all the benefits given to the pakeha. To make any progress against the Maoris' diffident inferiority complex and lack of education even more assistance had to be given them, and it had to be given with an understanding which would also help educate them in the ways of pakeha living. At the same time, this had to be done without depriving them of their own cultural heritage, from which pakeha New Zealanders might well learn a great deal. The Labour Government consciously went back to pick up the threads of Grey's policy towards the Maori; the final aim was to give him not merely the equal legal standing with the pakeha which he had possessed for a long time, but also an equality of opportunity. It was a vision of a bi-racial society living without stress or discrimination of any kind — a vision which has not yet been fulfilled, but at least both races have caught a glimpse of it. Indeed, as early as 1929 it had been decided to finance Maori land development from public moneys, and Royal Commissions in the twenties had examined Maori grievances — among them the injustice of many of the land confiscations after the Maori Wars. Wiremu Kingi was at last publicly exonerated. The Labour Government pushed the land schemes ahead with vigour and alacrity, directly assisting at least a fifth of the Maori population to better living standards. The Department of Maori Affairs greatly accelerated expenditure on Maori education and tremendous care and attention was given to the problem of Maori housing, the key, in so many cases, to better health among the Maori people. The Maoris never forgot their debt to the Labour Party and all four Maori seats remain Labour strongholds to this day.

Labour's next term of government was an unhappy one. Within the party itself a rift appeared between back-benchers and their leaders, as Fraser, growing old, irritable and domineering, relied more and more on the strength of the party machine to keep the Government functioning smoothly. A militant upsurge by some of the stronger Trade Unions left Fraser harassed and perplexed. Generally, he relied upon the firm support of the President of the Federation of Labour to control this half of the Labour camp, which, in the long run, he did, but it would have been fruitless to deny the growing industrial unrest. This proved a good target for Opposition criticism. New Zealand farmers and businessmen become understandably edgy when industrial dissent threatens the flow of goods, especially when the troubles concern the waterfront. Already ship turn-about in New Zealand ports was notoriously slow and ship owners were inclined to avoid docking where expensive delays might occur over trivial disputes. The Watersiders Union became more demanding and more obstructive until by 1949 it was clear that a showdown was inevitable.

With a dissatisfied country at home, Fraser was deeply concerned with New Zealand abroad. By 1949 the cold war was well under way, but the world had not yet settled down to this new element in international relations. The Berlin crisis had underlined the intransigence of the Russians and their destructive activities in the United Nations Security Council made smaller countries very fearful of another test of strength in which they would be crushed between the giants. The race for weapons was on, and with American atomic tests in the Pacific it seemed as if New Zealand's comfortable distance from the centre of world affairs might not be sufficient to save it again. Fraser was determined that New Zealand should have its own defensive force and pushed the issue of compulsory military training through a reluctant party by promising to put the question to referendum. In one of his less creditable moments, he used the machinery of Government to help swing public opinion towards the decision he wanted. It is ironic that a subsequent Labour Government abolished the system he established on the grounds that modern warfare required such intensively trained troops that only a regular army could supply them.

The 1949 election put the National Party in power. Holland fought the election on the rising cost of living, promising to make the pound go further and to release the country from its stifling network of controls. New Zealanders are essentially a pragmatic people who become impatient with an ultra-controlled existence only when it makes life inconvenient. This point had arrived and Holland removed the artificial brakes on prices and imports. Food subsidies were reduced and property sales were progressively freed from control. The result was immediate inflation as every interest in the country took advantage of its golden opportunity. The Government quickly restored food subsidies and price control, and increased monetary social security benefits to keep pace with rising prices. If anything, the pound was going an even shorter distance than before.

In the meantime, the waterfront issue had blown up into open conflict. In 1950 the Watersiders made a bid to dominate the Federation of Labour. They were dissatisfied with the Federation's function of promoting and protecting 'the freedom of the people and their political, social, economic and cultural welfare', and wished to return to the purer milk of unwatered socialist doctrine. Having failed to arouse the union moderates, the Watersiders set up a rival federation, the Trade Union Congress, which talked largely about nationalisation of the means of production, an equal share of the national wealth for all workers and the end of compulsory arbitration. Behind the fiery speeches, the real issue lay in a challenge of power to the Government. When the final moment came in 1951 the Government was more than ready. The Watersiders found themselves locked out and men from the armed forces were brought in to work the wharves under strong police protection. Only two unions came out in sympathy with the Watersiders; general feeling ran against a small group attempting to hold the economy to ransom. Slowly new waterfront unions, affiliated to the Federation, were formed and, growing stronger, took over from the soldiers on the wharves. The strike disintegrated, the workers trickled slowly over to the new unions and so to work.

The Government had proved itself tough and determined in this crisis, and the people approved of its actions. Accordingly, Holland, a shrewd politician alarmed at the rapidly increasing inflation, called for a snap election to vindicate Government in the face of Labour criticisms over the conduct of the strike. (Fraser had retired in 1949 and Nash was the new Labour leader.) The Government was well supported in the election, as it might not have been in the following year, and Holland immediately introduced a Police Offences Bill to provide legal machinery for coping with future industrial insurgents. Here, however, he mistook the temper of the country. The Labour Government had taken to itself extraordinarily wide powers during the war in order to organise the country's resources more efficiently. Even today some of these measures seem far-fetched and over-extensive, but it is generally agreed that in wartime a government cannot tolerate criticism verging on the subversive, and that it must, in the interests of the whole, interfere considerably with personal liberty. These measures had not been repealed at the end of the war, and were invoked by Holland in his fight against the Watersiders. He also introduced a new set of Emergency Regulations, justified to the country on the grounds that the Government was dealing with a clique of communists, rebellious ultra-socialists and protagonists of the cold war engaged in fifth column activities. Whatever may have been the truth of this, his new Bill went even further. It controlled the publication of 'seditious' matter, even in peacetime, and left the definition of sedition open to the vaguest interpretation. It made it an offence to criticise a Minister of the Crown. It also enlarged the powers of the police; a warrant was no longer necessary to search premises, and one clause gave a police constable authority to prevent access to roads or private property if he thought it necessary.

The New Zealander is not particularly concerned with the details of his personal liberty. He has always preferred his governments to provide egalitarian social security rather than defend his civil rights. He is more than ready to suffer considerable curtailment of personal liberty in order to ease the burden of his material anxieties. At the same time, though probably the most over-controlled citizen in the world, he possesses a deeply ingrained sense of personal authority which allows him to override controls whenever he feels they are unreasonable or inconvenient. In the Police Offences Bill the Government had gone too far. A public outcry defeated even the effective alliance between Government and newspapers, and Holland withdrew most of the objectionable clauses from the Bill. It is an interesting fact that many wartime emergency measures are still on the Statute Books and that in New Zealand, even the uncertain New Zealand of the future, it is unlikely that they will be abused.

In 1952 the Government faced yet another balance of payments crisis, and this in spite of the boom in wool prices due to the Korean War. Importers had bought and bought, and the country was close to dishonouring its overseas commitments. Instead of import licences, the Government restricted exchange allocations to importers in an effort to build up overseas reserves. The New Zealand economy since the war had been so prone to this sort of financial crisis that some people began to explore less orthodox economic theories. Enough support was given the Social Credit Party, preaching a modified form of the miraculous Douglas Credit which had so interested depression farmers, in the 1954 elections to reduce National's majority considerably.

During his time as Prime Minister, Sidney Holland initiated a long overdue constitutional change by abolishing the Legislative Council, a second chamber which for many years had not affected at all the decisions of the House of Representatives. Holland maintained that a Chamber without a function was an anachronism in modern government which wasted more time than could be afforded. For the whole of his period in office, Holland acted as his own

Finance Minister, usually keeping very close to orthodox financial theory. Unfortunately, his health gave out towards the end of 1957, and the National Party thought it better for the leadership to be in younger hands. Accordingly at the National Party caucus Holland nominated K. J. Holyoake as leader in his stead. Holland was later knighted and died in 1961.

In 1957, the Labour Party gained a narrow victory at the polls and with a very small majority found, in its turn, that the ever-pressing balance of payments crisis demanded urgent attention. Arnold Nordmeyer, the new Finance Minister in Nash's Government, framed a Budget which approached the problem from the need to curtail spending within the country. The so-called 'Black Budget' has generally been judged economically sound but the electorate considered it politically inept. It was an orthodox attempt to restore economic balance after a burst of excessive public and private spending, in the form of higher direct and indirect taxes. These fell rather heavily on wage-earners and the Government's fate was sealed by the bitter criticism of the leader of the Federation of Labour. Relations between the industrial and political wings of the Labour Party have often been tense but personalities played a major part in the 1958 estrangement. Neither the Opposition nor the country forgave or forgot the 'Black Budget', which hit hard at the things people like doing in order to maintain the standard of the things they must do. The Labour Government was abruptly shown the road in 1960, since when New Zealand has been governed by a National Administration under K. J. Holyoake.

Since the first Liberal Government, the tenor of New Zealand's political development has never been in doubt. New Zealanders are a conservative people – conservative in the sense that they dislike change. It has taken two calamitous depressions to take them from the safe and known paths of government out into radical untried ways. Even then, the methods used to carry out the radical measures can hardly be called revolutionary – extreme Labour's great criticism of Walter Nash was his financial orthodoxy. Each time, however, the radical social policies expressed the New Zealander's belief in an equal chance for everybody to live a 'good' life. Conservative opposition to either Liberal or Labour did not indicate a desire for true blue Toryism, but merely the New Zealander's desire to keep and stabilise what had been gained, slowly improving upon it as the occasion arose. The Welfare State is well established in New

Zealand, and no government will be permitted to undo what has already been done, even though, as Lord Beveridge commented with some point, it is not an unmitigated blessing.

However, 'From the beginning there was a concern for social justice.' Thus wrote J. B. Condliffe, New Zealand's greatest economic historian, many years ago in discussing the origin of the Welfare State which in many ways epitomises the country. From a concern for social justice there soon arose the idea that the State should actively promote personal welfare and this idea has never weakened. Indeed it has strengthened to the point where the State is often thought to know better than its citizens what is best for them and their children. In any case the high level of taxation necessary to provide a wide range of social services for everyone at little or no direct cost makes it very difficult for any but the wealthiest members of the community to opt out of public health, education and other services even if they should want to. Most people appear to be reasonably content with this situation but there is little pressure for an extension of social services, which now compare unfavourably with those of some other countries, whereas New Zealand undoubtedly led the field in the early post-war period.

The final touches to the Welfare State were applied by Labour Governments in the late thirties and forties but the foundations were laid at the beginning of the century. Then and subsequently there has been a polarity of political viewpoint on the State's role in welfare services but all Governments have added to, rather than subtracted from, their inheritance in this field. The marked extension of State welfare services undertaken by the first Labour Government provoked acrimonious debates, the muted overtones of which can still be heard. Neither side has ever properly appreciated the good and bad points of the system and many of the arguments for and against have been vitiated by extravagant polemic. The Right's prophecies of moral degradation have been unfulfilled but equally the naïve utopian hopes of the Left have been disappointed. The basic strength and appeal of the Welfare State has always been the protection it afforded the individual against arbitrary and undeserved blows of fate; its greatest weakness an almost automatic erosion of the sense of personal responsibility. Apart from the personal insurance aspect, the motivation has been humanitarian rather than doctrinaire, pragmatic rather than systematic, with political opportunism playing its natural part from time to time. At the present time Government social services comprise substantially free medical benefits, drugs and hospitalisation, family benefits, old age benefits and universal superannuation, and the usual range of widows', orphans', sickness and unemployment benefits. Dental services except for schoolchildren are not free nor are optical services, and specialist medical costs are only met by the State to a minor extent unless a person is prepared to wait a long time for free attention at public hospitals. Education at State schools and higher institutions of learning is also free. The State also provides rental houses at low cost for people on low incomes. Generally the welfare system is a hotch-potch of generosity as with family benefits (no means test) and parsimony as with old age benefits where a means test is applied, and it abounds with anomalies such as the absence of any provision for raising State house rentals if the income of tenants increases. Occasionally near scandals occur as when a previous National Government eager to assert the virtues of private enterprise offered to sell State houses to their occupiers but at a price that permitted most to make a handsome tax-free capital gain.

Full employment policies are often looked upon as part of the Welfare State but they are logically and practically separate although those keenest on preserving full employment at any cost are generally strong supporters of public health and medicine and of generous social security benefits to the aged, the insecure and the infirm – not to mention the young. Perhaps naturally, unemployment benefits are not generous in New Zealand compared with other countries. So few people draw them that it is not an issue. Extensive Government intervention in normal business activities, such as banking, insurance, forestry, land settlement, mining, public utilities, transport and now steel, are also not necessarily part of a Welfare State but there is correlation. The concept of an active benevolent State intervening in economic and social affairs outside the area of traditional action such as law, order and defence, also finds extensive expression in New Zealand's maze of Government regulatory functions. Faith in the State's conscience as well as benevolence has been somewhat shaken in the post-war period by its evident failure to maintain economic stability and a satisfactory growth rate but residual support of vested interest has so far resisted any significant dismantling of controls. The greatest danger to welfare services in the narrow sense probably lies in the common equation of them with controls in the economic sphere which are not nearly so obviously advantageous to the community as a whole although they undoubtedly assist particular groups of people. Government regulation in the interests of national welfare so easily becomes regulation for the benefit of vested interests; certainly change is inhibited for public servants as well as Ministers naturally prefer the *status quo* to anything else.

New Zealand Governments now face an economic problem of some magnitude. Throughout the post-war period the country's problems have been largely of its own making, as export prices have continued to rise in a very satisfactory manner. However, it is impossible to ignore the threat of what would happen should prices fall. With nearly all the eggs in one large basket, everyone in the country is affected by the state of world markets for these products. A country with little known mineral potential, the land will probably remain New Zealand's major asset, but the time has arrived to diversify the end products of farming and perhaps deliberately expand some non-farming activities, such as forestry. Also, it is time to consider with less abandon than in the past the need to develop secondary industries and to decide which ones they should be. A haphazard encouragement and protection of all secondary industries has led to a plethora of small, uneconomic ventures, producing goods which generally retail at higher prices than similar imported products. Quality also has frequently been neglected. It is apparent that some industries based on agricultural products, such as the leather industry which is at present quite marginal, should be built up, while at the same time the activities of woollen mills should be closely scrutinised. All this is obvious enough; what is not obvious is which heavy industries should be established, because, like Japan, all raw materials will have to be imported. To have any great effect, the goods from these industries should be able to compete in their own right with overseas prices.

The problem of New Zealand's apparent inability to maintain adequate overseas reserves while at the same time preventing domestic inflation is further complicated by the nature of New Zealand society, very reluctant to sacrifice in one direction to achieve more in another. The history of the post-war years is almost exclusively an economic history; all far-reaching events have originated in the financial state of the country. New Zealanders have shown a consistent desire not only to live right up to their income, but generally beyond it. Politicians have proved unable to refuse sectional demands which in total have led to excessive spending, leading in turn to a level of importing the country could not afford. The welfare pro-visions which play such a large part in New Zealand's way of life have reduced the desire or the need to save. This has all been very pleasant while it lasted and at the time of writing few New Zea-landers are ready to agree that it must stop. It is still the Govern-ment's job to do something if things are as bad as 'they' say. As one government and then another has failed to produce a solution to the problem – one that would build up overseas resources and at the same time allow a high spending rate – more and more people have begun to explore a theory which seems to have the answer up its sleeve. Social Credit, departing further and further from its original policy with the passage of time, gained substantial increased support in 1957 when the balance of payments problems became significantly pressing. Social Credit's most loyal adherents are to be found in the poorer farming communities; in all except financial matters it is an ultra right-wing party, considerably more so than the National Party itself, and perhaps bears a close resemblance to Massey's early Reform Party. As economic conditions temporarily improved, the party's support fell, but rose with a jump during the 1966 elections when the Labour Party under its inexperienced leader Norman Kirk made little effort to do more than hold its own. Social Credit voters reduced the National majority considerably, though they made little impression on Labour's election figures. For the first time a member of the party was elected to Parliament; whether this is significant or not probably depends upon the shape of New Zealand's economic future.

One thing which can be safely predicted is that New Zealand's political institutions will continue to reflect the sectional interests of the country's society. Because of the original homogeneity of the settlers, mostly lower middle-class stock, New Zealand has ex-perienced very few class struggles. Government has usually been with an eye to the main vested interests in the community – one outrageous example of this was the News Media Bill which was rushed through Parliament to prevent Lord Thomson's takeover of a particularly inefficient pro-Government newspaper. However, although the system has its disadvantages it is infinitely to be pre-ferred to one where political parties represent distinct class divisions.

New Zealand's role in external affairs has remained very much in the pattern established by Peter Fraser, although some of the early independent vigour has worn a little thin. As a member of the

United Nations New Zealand sent troops to Korea when it was invaded. This was so much a test case of all that the United Nations stood for, and so worthy of support from a small, equally vulnerable country, that there was no lack of volunteers for 'K' force. In the United Nations New Zealand often took an independent course from that of Britain – it stands to its eternal credit that it did not abstain over the Israel issue, but voted for the creation of the Jewish state.

Although it remains a firm member of the Commonwealth, New Zealand has had to establish for itself a complex series of alliances with an eye to defence in South-east Asia and the Pacific. New Zealand acts in the South Pacific usually in consultation with Australia, although perhaps the time has arrived for more active independent policies in this area. It has been very easy to let Australia and Britain carry most of the burden of financial assistance to the islands of the South Pacific, but New Zealand has a greater community of interest with many of them than has Australia, if only by the presence within New Zealand of a Polynesian culture. Education at all levels is the crying need of the islands and New Zealand could do much more to help in this sphere. She administers some of the smaller Pacific islands, but this is an insignificant contribution; the Cook Island group and Western Samoa have both been granted independence, with New Zealand acting for them in foreign affairs.

Both Australia and New Zealand have recognised the overriding importance of the United States in all Pacific affairs. America is the rock upon which all New Zealand's policy in South-east Asia and the Pacific is firmly anchored. In 1951 New Zealand signed the ANZUS treaty with Australia and the United States, a treaty aimed mostly at creating an alliance in the case of future Japanese aggression. Fortunately, Japan has proved more interested in trading than in hostility.

In 1954 New Zealand joined the new South-East Asia Treaty Organisation (SEATO) in company with Australia, France, Pakistan, the Philippines, Thailand, the United Kingdom and the United States. The main articles of SEATO provide for help to any member of the organisation if attacked, and extend this promise of help also to certain designated countries – viz. free Vietnam, Laos and Cambodia. New Zealand has endeavoured to concentrate upon the peaceful aspects of SEATO, offering under its terms different kinds of educational and technical assistance. However, as a signatory to

SEATO, New Zealand in 1955 supplied armed forces to fight in Malaya during the Emergency and again during Confrontation. New Zealand troops are now fighting in Vietnam, even though this conflict is as disturbing and distressing to New Zealanders as it is to most other peoples. New Zealand is also a participant in the Colombo Plan, which provides help for underdeveloped countries in the form of capital projects, technical assistance and educational opportunities. The Colombo Plan is a recognition that unless backward countries are helped to the prosperity they can see in Western societies, they may well become dangerous neighbours. It is an attempt to begin at the beginning of peaceful international relations.

One of the most obvious spheres of New Zealand's involvement with its neighbours is that of trade, especially since the threat of British entry into the European Economic Community. South-east Asian countries are not particularly interested in New Zealand's primary produce, although Japan is providing an increasing market for meat, but they have in common with it the necessity to export. By encouraging economic development in Thailand, Malaysia and Indonesia, New Zealand is helping to build potential markets for itself. Under the United Nations scheme of regional assistance, New Zealand in ECAFE (Economic Commission for Asia and the Far East) is contributing to the development of productive projects in this area. The assistance given by ECAFE to underdeveloped countries might well do more towards establishing a faster economic growth and hence a desire for peaceful trading relations than any security measure. In South-east Asia the work of ECAFE is frequently dovetailed into that of FAO (the Food and Agricultural Organisation of the United Nations) of which New Zealand is also a member.

The future must bring to New Zealand a reassessment of technical assistance to underdeveloped countries. Much has been learnt about the techniques of assistance to protect the giver from an appearance of condescension and the recipient from embarrassment. The United States Peace Corps Movement has made a big impression in South-east Asia, because its members are prepared to work alongside the local people and are not merely advisers. Along with other countries like Germany, Britain and Israel, New Zealand also has its Volunteer Service Abroad movement, only partially supported by the State. It is becoming increasingly evident that the way to world peace lies along these paths. New Zealand is an affluent country by any standards; it gives less than one quarter of one per cent of its national income to this sort of activity. Up until now, it has been possible to coast along in the shadow cast by the generosity of the United States, but in the name of New Zealand's traditional liberal humanitarianism, if not in sheer self-interest, the contribution must be increased to a more reasonable amount. Israel, with the same population as New Zealand, makes much greater efforts in this field, offering advanced education to many more Africans than our Colombo Plan scheme gives to Asians. New Zealand's armed forces might be limited and its commitments in this direction therefore small, but its technical skills and educational opportunities are great. The time has come to share them more generously and with a wider understanding of the problems of underdeveloped countries. This is not an exercise in international charity, but rather a further step in New Zealand's growing realisation of what it means to be involved in the world.

Chapter 6

Economic and Administrative Structure

HISTORICALLY, primary industry has been New Zealand's mainstay; this is as true today as it ever was although fewer and fewer people have any direct connection with the land. The cow and the sheep together have almost literally been the basis of high living standards in the past and this is still the case, although the connection is more indirect. To put the matter in a nutshell: no other country of any size has such a high ratio of exports to total production nor such a high proportion of exports in the form of primary products. In its land orientation New Zealand is more akin to underdeveloped countries than to highly industrialised Western powers. Indeed the derogatory phrase 'England's overseas farm' has been used by advocates of more secondary industry to sum up New Zealand's 'neo-colonial economic status'. This is now rather misleading as considerable progress has been made recently in diversifying both products and markets but there is enough truth in it to justify anxiety about the consequences of the United Kingdom joining the European Economic Community. Certainly, the protectionism practised by Common Market countries in favour of their own farmers is inimical to temperate producers and exporters of farm products.

For the present anyway, grasslands farming is the linchpin of the New Zealand economy with other segments of primary industry-forestry – mining, fishing, arable farming and fruit and vegetable growing – in a subordinate role. The analysis of New Zealand's export earnings in 1966 given below is illuminating; it shows a re-markable – some would say reckless – concentration on a narrow range of pastoral products. This is unquestionably risky but concentration and specialization also have well-known advantages; New Zealand farmers are more prosperous than in most countries and there is a smaller difference between urban and rural living standards. In fact the majority of farmers enjoy higher incomes, in cash and in kind, than the generality of urban workers.

Export Earnings in 1966

	£ million	per cent
Dairy products	108	26
Meat	106	26
Wool	124	30
Other animal products	36	9
Forest products	13	3
Other primary products	15	4
Miscellaneous products	8	2
Total export receipts	410	100

Some of the added value incorporated in exports is of course attributable to manufacturing and service activities rather than to primary industry and a better insight into the structure of the economy is afforded by the recent inter-industry study. The following table is a condensed version, showing for 1959–60 the main linkages between sectors as well as their relative importance. Primary industry includes the main processing industries, e.g. dairy factories, meat works, fruit and vegetable preserving, woollen milling, sawmills and pulp- and paper-mills as well as the primary activities themselves. Construction, transport etc. includes public utilities such as gas, electricity and communications.

Reading from left to right in the table overleaf one sees the distribution of each sector's output both to other productive sectors and to final use. Thus primary industry in 1959–60 sold to the rest of the economy and abroad goods worth £453 million, of which no less than £279 million was accounted for by exports. Sales to consumers totalled £91 million, and the industry produced capital goods worth £9 million for use by itself or other sectors. A similar interpretation applies to the other rows in the table. In each case sales to consumers have been valued net of indirect taxation and subsidies to give a more accurate picture of each sector's output. The added value row shows the origin of national income, the depreciation row contains estimates of the capital erosion resulting from production, and the imports row is self-explanatory.

Reading down the columns, one sees each sector's cost structure or pattern of purchases. The column for consumption expenditure combines consumer purchases (net of indirect taxes and subsidies) and public authority current expenditure. The next column combines fixed capital expenditure and changes in stocks, including livestock. Exports are the last final demand category.

Inter-industry Structure of New Zealand Economy

£ million 1959/60 — Sales of / Purchases by	Primary industry	Manufacturing	Construction, etc.	Distribution, etc.	Services, etc.	Consumption	Capital formation	Exports	TOTAL
Primary industry	—	27	34	2	11	91	9	279	453
Manufacturing	46	—	58	16	13	184	55	14	386
Construction, transport, etc.	35	34	—	24	16	71	177	25	383
Distribution and finance	29	30	27	—	8	161	19	15	289
Services and administration	5	8	5	25	—	233	7	5	288
Added value	285	174	212	199	214	—	—	—	1084
Depreciation	27	15	23	16	18	—	—	—	99
Imports	26	98	24	7	8	75	40	2	280
TOTAL	453	386	383	289	288	815	307	341	—

The top left quadrant of the table gives the inter-industry pattern of sales and purchases underlying the generation of national income, equal in 1959–60 to £1,084 million. The bottom left quadrant shows the imports and factor inputs required and the top right quadrant the pattern of final demand. The bottom right quadrant shows that £75 million worth of imports were consumption goods in a substantially finished state, imports used directly in capital formation were valued at £40 million, and the value of goods imported for re-export was £2 million. (In inter-industry tables of this sort, wholesale and retail distribution services are shown as margins, along with transport costs.)

The apparent net foreign exchange earnings of the primary sector in 1959–60 were £253 million and similarly for the other sectors but this ignores inter-industry linkages. Thus the manufacturing sector imported a good deal on behalf of other sectors. Nevertheless the contribution of the primary sector and its associated processing facilities to New Zealand's foreign exchange earnings is overwhelming.

The sector's substantial contribution to national productivity is shown by the following comparison between added value and employment. Here primary produce processing industries are perforce shown along with other manufacturing.

Sector 1959–60	Added Value £m	%	Employment 000	%
Primary industry	223	21	141	16
Manufacturing	236	22	220	25
Construction, transport, etc.	212	19	178	21
Distribution and finance	199	18	148	17
Services and administration	214	20	181	21
Whole economy	1084	100	868	100

The relatively high added value per person in primary industry is also a reflection of heavy capitalisation in farming, forestry and mining and the predominance of male workers. In manufacturing the large number of female workers and prevalence of small units are factors contributing to a relatively low average added value per worker. In the case of construction, transport, communications and utilities, the main reason for the discrepancy between added value and employment is the high proportion of unskilled jobs in the industry.

So much for the broad structure of the economy. The following pages deal with the main aspects in more detail. One important fact should be borne in mind all the time: New Zealand has enjoyed full employment throughout the post-war period. Thus in 1960, unemployment was under 1,000 – one-tenth of one per cent of the labour force. People in other countries find such a low level of unemployment incredible; younger New Zealanders have never known anything else.

Most New Zealand farms are worked by their owners, often with the assistance of families but with little or no permanent hired labour, partly because suitable labour is simply not available. Shearing is however traditionally done by itinerant gangs and an increasing amount of other farm work is now undertaken by contractors – aerial topdressing and sowing being a notable example. Family farming is the rule in dairying and fat lamb farming but hired labour is of course necessary on the larger sheep stations. In the North Island, especially, some beef cattle are generally run with sheep, mainly to improve pasture control.

Roughly a quarter of all farms are leased, often from the State, but three-fifths are freehold. In dairying a proportion are worked on a share basis, the owner providing land and improvements, and the share-milker generally supplying the herd. This affords a way for men without much capital to acquire a farm which today may be worth anything from ten to twenty times the average income of the community. Sheep farms, being larger as a rule, are normally worth considerably more. With the trend towards company farming it is now possible for more men to embark on a farming career as managers. Such men are often graduates of agricultural colleges; many other graduates find employment as farm advisers with the Department of Agriculture or specialised agencies.

Improved techniques and extensive use of fertilisers have led to a marked increase in farm output since the war with virtually no change in area farmed and an appreciable fall in employment. Heavy investment in mechanisation has of course been necessary to achieve this. Livestock numbers have increased substantially but productivity per beast has also risen. The yield of milk and wool is now very high and the lambing percentage has also improved. Technological change in sheep husbandry has not always, however, had beneficial results. As wool yields have increased through purposeful breeding, second shearing and greater availability of grass, the fibres have become shorter and coarser, and it is this type of wool that is in least demand today. Efforts to increase the quantity and quality of lamb and mutton have also had adverse effects on the quality of wool.

Arable farming has traditionally been eclipsed by grasslands farming because the latter was more profitable but the recent fall in lamb and wool prices has boosted wheat acreages to the extent that the country is now nearly self-sufficient in wheat after many years of heavy importing.

Grass seed, tobacco and hops have long been produced in suitable areas and more recently the popularity of frozen vegetables has given an incentive for more cash crop farming. No sugar beet is currently grown but the possibility of this crop has been investigated and even rice is being considered. Supplementary fodder crops are grown to a limited extent, mainly in the South Island, but in most places pasture growth is continuous throughout the year and there is not much need for fodder crops. Hay and ensilage are the main supplementary stock foods.

1   Captain William Hobson, R.N.
(1795–1842)

2   Sir George Edward Grey
(1812–1898)

3   Sir Harry Albert Atkinson
(1831–1892)

4   Sir Julius Vogel (1835–99)

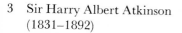

5 John Ballance (1839–93)

6 Richard John ('King Dick') Seddon (1845–1906)

7 Sir Joseph George Ward, Bart. (1857–1930)

8 William Ferguson Massey (1856–1925)

9 Cob Farmhouse, Otago, built in the early 1850s

10 Residency of Edward Gibbon Wakefield, Principal Agent of
    the New Zealand Company, Wellington, 1841–45

11 Watercolour of Wellington in 1841 by Charles Heaphy

12 The *Dunedin*, the first refrigerated cargo ship, which sailed
from Port Chalmers in February 1882

14 Katherine Mansfield (Mrs John Middleton Murry; 1888–1923)

13 A two-storeyed wooden house built in 1890 and showing restrained Gothic ornamentation

15 The Labour Party Cabinet, 1935. *Left to right:* Robert Semple, Hubert Thomas Armstrong, Frederick Jones, Daniel Giles Sullivan, Patrick Charles Webb, Mark Fagan, H. G. R. Mason, Walter Nash, William Edward Parry, Frank Langstone, Michael Joseph

16   Troops landing at Anzac Cove, Dardanelles, April 1915

17   Joseph Gordon Coates (1878–1943) with members of the Maori
      rugby team during his visit to England in 1926

19 Lt. General Lord Freyberg (1890–1963) in 1954

18 Sir Sidney Holland (1893–1961; *left*) arriving at 10 Downing Street, London, with Sir William Jordan, New Zealand High Commissioner, for the Commonwealth Prime Ministers Conference in 1951

20   The Octagon, Dunedin

21   St Paul's Cathedral, Wellington

22   Queen Street, Auckland

23   Aerial view of Christchurch

24   Auckland as seen through Auckland harbour bridge

25   Tree ferns and Nikau palms in Waipoua Forest, Northland

26   Kaingaroa State Forest, Auckland Province, showing the new
Kawerau–Murupara railway along the edge of the trees

27   Ohope Beach, Whakatane, Auckland Province

28   Aerial view of Wairakei Hotel and Geothermal Valley,
Auckland Province

29   Dairy herd of Jersey cows on a farm at Rukuhia, Hamilton

30 Aerial view of Tasman Pulp and Paper Mills, Kawerau, Auckland Province

31 Mohaka River Bridge, North Island

32　Aerial view of Taranaki, with Mount Egmont in the background.

33　Mitre Peak, Milford Sound, Southland

Arrangements for processing and marketing farm produce vary greatly. In the case of dairying, processing is carried out by co-operative factories, sometimes organised as groups, but marketing is handled by the Dairy Board, both overseas and in New Zealand. This industry organisation is a statutory agency enjoying very favourable borrowing terms from the Reserve Bank although dairy factories themselves bank locally with commercial banks. The Board is responsible for both herd and product quality and research but its main function is marketing and it is able to exercise considerable leverage on dairy factories to ensure that the product mix is well suited to market demand. Thus in recent years steady encouragement has been given to diversification of production towards casein, milk powders and condensed milk. Tanker collection of milk from farms is now the rule and many factories possess dual plants so that production may be switched quickly to meet changing market conditions. A guaranteed price scheme operates in respect of butterfat used in the manufacture of butter and cheese. Short run fluctuations in industry funds are financed by the Reserve Bank but this stabilisation arrangement is operated with long term balance as the aim.

The Meat Board administers a floor price scheme but this body has far less control over the pastoral industry, especially as a separate Wool Board also exists. There is very little justification, except historical accident, for having two such Boards; sheep after all grow both meat and wool. A very severe setback to the pastoral industry would, however, be required to effect a merger. The slaughter of livestock for export is carried out very largely by companies, which also handle marketing overseas, but farmers may have their stock killed on commission and export the meat themselves. Stock for local consumption is commonly processed in abattoirs operated by local authorities. Slaughter for export is of course a highly seasonal occupation, traditionally an avenue for students to earn money to help keep themselves during the following year. Meat consumption in New Zealand is very high but almost all in the form of beef, mutton and pork. Lamb consumption is very low, practically the whole of the lamb kill being exported, particularly to the United Kingdom. Local beef consumption, however, is roughly half total production and in the case of pig meats the whole of it.

New Zealand has had woollen mills since the very early days but woollen milling has not thrived, mainly because of a failure to specialise. The amount of wool processed locally is therefore minimal. Wool marketing is by auction but recently the merits of this system have been seriously questioned. Oddly enough the Wool Board has no marketing function; the floor price scheme being operated by another statutory body known as the Wool Commission. Now that the Commission owns a lot of wool, passed to it during the 1966–67 season because of a slump in coarse wools, it may be able to initiate overdue changes in marketing. The separation of function between Wool Board and Wool Commission is even harder to justify than the separate existence of the Meat Board and the Wool Board.

There are also regulatory and marketing agencies for other primary products, and town milk producers are paid an allowance for the extra costs of producing milk all the year round. The obvious cost-reducing device of reconstituting milk from powder in the off season has yet to be tried. Producer co-operatives have proved themselves in milk processing but attempts to extend the co-operative principle to other activities associated with farming have proved less successful. Co-operative meat freezing works, fertiliser works, wool marketing agencies and stock and station agencies all exist but they tend to be overshadowed by corporate enterprises or to operate like them.

Hunting has never been a serious business in New Zealand and today it is in the main a recreation or control activity. The hunting of wild pigs is a traditional sport in the wilder parts of the country and deer stalking is also popular. Both animals were of course introduced into the country; the latter deliberately to provide game, the former as farm animals. Serious efforts are now being made to exterminate red deer which inhibit forest regeneration and thereby aggravate soil conservation problems. Rabbits and opossums are also noxious animals in New Zealand conditions and continual efforts are necessary to limit their numbers in order to minimise damage to farmlands and native bush.

The sea surrounding New Zealand abounds with fish but fishing, although almost the country's first industry, has not thrived as might have been expected. For the Maoris fish were of course the main source of protein but today fish consumption is low by world standards. Freshwater fishing is a sport, not a business, and the introduction of table fish such as are common in Europe and Asia is opposed lest they prey upon the trout found in most lakes and streams but which really have little economic value. Big game fishing off the northern coasts is similarly significant only as a recreation activity and tourist attraction.

Whaling was an important activity in the early nineteenth century but today it is no more, due to over-'fishing' mainly by whalers of other nationalities. Trawling for table fish is mainly for the local market, but efforts to increase wet fish exports have been intensified in recent years. At present, however, the main exports are of crayfish. Oddly enough, oyster exports are prohibited – oysters being widely regarded as a Kiwi's perquisite. To date there have been no systematic efforts to establish oyster farms. Shellfish generally are under-exploited but, with the advent of cheap air freighting, these and other high-value fish may offer more attractive commercial possibilities in future. Lack of initiative in catching fish is paralleled by an archaic distribution system. Clearly fishing is an industry with a future but not as it is presently organised.

When European settlers arrived in New Zealand, bush covered almost all the North Island and an appreciable area of indigenous forest remains. The long life cycle of the native trees, however, greatly reduces their economic potential. Today there are also several large exotic forests, especially of radiata pine, planted mainly in the 1920's and 1930's, and these trees are now being extensively milled for timber, pulp, Kraft paper and newsprint. Only the wetter western parts of the South Island were ever heavily afforested and there are still large stands of beech but generally in inaccessible spots. Exotic forests are also found in the South Island but not always in suitable places, as was shown a few years ago when high winds caused havoc in one planted on light soil. Despite the depredations of systematic settlement, forest still accounts for over a fifth of New Zealand's land area but only a quarter is commercially usable.

The aims of the New Zealand Forest Service, established in 1920, are to conserve and perpetuate indigenous forests and 'to create an exotic estate large enough and sufficiently diverse to supply the future needs of New Zealand in timber and other forest produce and to cater for export markets'. In the case of indigenous forests, a major motive for conservation is prevention of soil erosion in high country and water regulation generally. The prospects of perpetuating most native species appear good. In the case of exotic forests, the problem at the present time is mainly to ensure that there is sufficient processing capacity and adequate export markets to keep up with the growth of radiata pine which in New Zealand conditions displays tremendous vitality.

In the last fifteen years roundwood production has more than doubled but output of sawn timber has increased by only 50 per cent, with exotic species accounting for two-thirds of the sawn timber but a much higher proportion of total fellings. In this period wood pulp production has increased ten times and New Zealand is now a significant producer and exporter of pulp and newsprint. There are two major pulp and paper mills – one entirely private enterprise, the other a joint venture between the State, two large overseas paper groups, a leading New Zealand company and the general public. This unusual consortium uses trees from a large State forest and was in fact formed for this purpose. Its principal product at present is newsprint but proposals to install a Kraft machine for export to Australia have been announced, incidentally subjecting the recently arranged Limited Free Trade Agreement with that country (negotiated in 1965) to its first test. The other major pulp and paper mill specialises in production for the local market. Both firms produce large quantities of sawn timber.

Nearly 40,000 people are presently employed in the forestry industry as a whole, double the number twenty years ago, and capital investment since the war has been heavy. Besides reducing New Zealand's imports of timber and other wood products, this expansion has resulted in considerable foreign exchange earnings. Without doubt forestry is destined to become even more important in the future as the country is very well suited to the growing of trees which today represent an important alternative use for large areas of land, New Zealand's historic foundation.

Although New Zealand is geologically complex and has a wide variety of minerals, few deposits of economic significance have so far been discovered. Gold is of course an exception but even this was relatively quickly worked out. Substantial deposits of coal exist but it is mostly of inferior grade and not mined efficiently or extensively. There are, however, vast reserves of iron sand on the west coast beaches of both islands and New Zealand's first full-scale steel mill based upon them will be in operation by 1968.

Efforts to locate oil in profitable quantities have so far been unsuccessful. Systematic exploration was begun many years ago but the only strike to date proved to be gas. The oil quest is tantalising as several small wells at New Plymouth, commissioned at the beginning of the century, are still producing. The natural gas discovered in south Taranaki in 1959 will yield a considerable quantity of petroleum as condensate when the proposed pipe lines to Auckland and Wellington are completed.

Just as oil seepages at New Plymouth first excited interest in petroleum exploration, so the possibilities of commercial utilisation of geothermal steam were suggested by the great natural thermal activity in and about Wairakei in the centre of the North Island. After many difficulties, geothermal steam has now been successfully harnessed for electricity generation. This is a far cry from kauri gum, New Zealand's first 'mineral' resource to be systematically exploited.

Mining began in New Zealand soon after organised European settlement, or long before it if Maori expeditions to secure 'greenstone' are included. This was found in Westland and used for weapons, tools and ornaments. The first European mining was for manganese and copper near Auckland and in Otago. This never proved very successful and only lately, as a result of increases in world prices, has interest in this type of mining revived. Copper ore, for example, is quite widely distributed but not in workable lodes.

Although the search for base metals in New Zealand has been largely fruitless, the country is well endowed with important non-metallic minerals such as clay, limestone, sand and gravel used to make agricultural lime, cement and glass. Other minerals of importance are serpentine (a low-grade phosphatic rock) for fertiliser production and salt from a lake by the coast on the north east of the South Island where the wind nearly always blows, the sun nearly always shines and the rainfall is extraordinarily low. Industrial salt has been produced for some years and table salt is now being mooted. Asbestos and uranium deposits also exist.

Historically the main coalfields were just south of Auckland and in Westland. Whereas the former are well situated near the industrial heart of New Zealand, the latter have suffered from their isolation and are on the decline. Open cast methods are now being used extensively in the South Auckland field to supply a thermal power station, and shortly the new steel works which will be only a few miles away.

The most important primary produce processing industries have been mentioned already. Dairy factories have undergone extensive mechanisation in recent years and their productivity is high. It has not so far been found possible or desirable to automate livestock slaughter and processing to the same extent and productivity in meat works has shown no substantial improvement for a long time. Some rationalisation of meat processing has, however, resulted from the closing down of a few small works. Processing is now being carried somewhat further than used to be the case in an effort to increase sales of lamb, especially in North America, and much greater emphasis has been laid on hygienic handling of both beef and lamb in recent years.

Vegetable processing, first canning and now quick freezing, has made great strides in recent years, peas being the main but by no means the only crop. This industry is centred on Hastings and Gisborne, two of the few areas in New Zealand where there is rich soil. A substantial export trade with Australia has been built up over the years and frozen vegetables are included in the Limited Free Trade Agreement. In contrast with this growth industry, grain milling, one of the country's earliest manufacturing activities, is almost static. Flour milling in most years is dependent on imports from Australia and for this reason is not included with other primary produce processing industries in the table at the beginning of this chapter. The other food processing industry based on local produce handles fruit and this centres on the east coast of the North Island but also in Nelson and Central Otago.

Woollen milling was established in New Zealand as early as the eighteen-seventies but this industry has never succeeded in building up an export market nor in satisfying local requirements. In attempting to achieve the latter, without rationalising production, the former has been sacrificed because the New Zealand market is not large enough to permit numerous competing firms to produce a wide range of goods economically. Very recently a box manufacturer has acquired several mills and a thorough reorganisation seems likely, including 'top' manufacture on a large scale. The remaining industries in the primary produce processing group are engaged in converting logs into sawn timber, pulp, paper and other wood products. These industries have already been discussed as regards their main products. Besides them, however, there is now a much more diverse range of minor products – veneers, plywoods, parquets and the like.

Manufacturing versus farming has been a constant subject of debate since the war but this issue will be discussed in the chapter following. For present purposes it is enough to note that under the protection of import licensing, first imposed in 1938, there has been a marked expansion of manufacturing based mainly on imported raw materials. The New Zealand manufacturing sector is now similar in composition to that of most other small Western countries but with a notable absence to date of basic metal and chemical industries. Some industries of course are closely linked with farming, such as fertiliser works which use imported sulphur to convert imported phosphate rock into soluble phosphates to compensate for the marked phosphate deficiency of most New Zealand soils. Another such industry is lime manufacture and a fast growing one produces insecticides, stock remedies, etc. The manufacture of agricultural machinery has been carried out in New Zealand very efficiently for a long time and there is an export trade in some such products. The country has of course the normal complement of industries producing goods for the local market for which import substitutes are not possible or very expensive because of transport costs.

Motor vehicle assembly plants were built in New Zealand prior to World War II and a number of other important consumer goods industries were in existence by then. The war stimulated many light-heavy industries and protective policies since the war have encouraged a very wide range of light industry almost entirely focused on the local market. Since these are such as are found elsewhere, attention will be directed to recent developments tending towards more heavy industry. The most notable example is the steel mill now being built to utilise local iron sands, coal and electricity. A small merchant bar mill is already in operation based on scrap and the two between them will satisfy New Zealand's requirements of basic steel products for some time to come.

A number of heavy metal fabricating industries have also been established since the war but one long-standing one – the Railway workshops – has suffered from shortage of labour to the extent that it has virtually ceased manufacture of rolling stock. There is now an aluminium fabricating plant and hopes are held for an aluminium smelter later on, based on imported bauxite but utilising the relatively abundant hydro-electric resources of the South Island. A notable recent addition to the country's heavy industry is an oil refinery with sufficient capacity to satisfy local requirements, but again the local resources for it are limited – being only the condensate that will be available from the Kapuni gas field when the gas is drawn off. Two other large plants built lately are a glass works and nylon spinning factory. New Zealand does not, however, produce the nylon polymer. A cotton mill was mooted and partly constructed some years ago but not proceeded with as a result of strenuous opposition from cotton textile importers and also from disinterested critics of an indiscriminate industrialisation policy.

The local raw materials or resources that cry out for further exploitation are fish, wool, trees and coal but in many cases the scale necessary for profitable operation is beyond the capacity of the New Zealand market, so production for export must be planned from the beginning in order to achieve a satisfactory level of productivity.

Building and construction is an industry with a disappointing productivity record. This was the first industry of all, if one includes the settlers' own efforts, and so far as house building is concerned technological progress would appear to have been minimal ever since. Most houses are still erected as entities with the assistance of few mass production techniques. Commercial building on the other hand has adapted itself better to a high wage-scarce labour economy and construction work is now highly mechanised. The utilisation of expensive capital equipment is not generally satisfactory, however.

Home building is typically the milieu of small builders although this is changing slowly, whereas big firms dominate the commercial field. In the case of construction, a large amount of work is undertaken by Government and local authorities but there are a number of large private contractors. Labour shortages in recent years have been such that penalty clauses have seldom been invoked for delays, sometimes inordinate, in completing large buildings and construction jobs. Unlike most other New Zealand business, the industry has experienced a number of minor recessions which have effected the disappearance of the least efficient firms. Another such 'shake-out' is now in progress. The typical small builder or contractor is grossly under-capitalised and some large ones also over-extend themselves; so they go bankrupt whenever jobs fail to succeed one another without delay, and sometimes even when they do.

Building and construction is one of the few remaining industries in which unskilled workers can find employment and the apprenticeship system, traditionally New Zealand's method of training tradesmen, has largely broken down. Whatever the cause, it is apparent that building costs in New Zealand are high, perhaps a quarter higher than one would expect in the light of costs overseas.

There has been a revolution in overseas passenger travel in the last decade or so, despite relatively high air fares. Today over 80 per cent of passengers entering or leaving New Zealand do so by air, many on the country's own (State) airline, Air New Zealand. A similar revolution in the carriage of valuable freight between countries is imminent but meanwhile sea-freight holds the stage. Because a high proportion of New Zealand's exports require refrigeration and are destined for the United Kingdom, the country is virtually bound to use the services of the so-called Conference Lines. There are frequent wrangles between the Producer Boards, representing New Zealand farmers, and the Conference Lines over freight rates but perhaps the most valid criticism of the shipping companies is not their exploitation of monopoly power but their lack of initiative and enterprise. On the other hand, efforts to streamline loading and unloading have not been impressive and the New Zealand waterfront is as bad as anywhere in the world for labour relations.

For internal transport the (State) Railways are still the mainstay, especially since the commissioning of inter-island rail ferries. Railway long-distance passenger traffic appears doomed but, as in other countries, rail is more economic than road transport for heavy long distance freight haulage. Pervasive transport licensing regulations have been in force for many years, ostensibly to rationalise internal transport, but really to protect the Railways. These regulations are now being relaxed as the need for them is less apparent with the Railways concentrating on wholesale haulage and leaving short-distance miscellaneous carriage to road transport operators. Air freight is becoming more and more widely used and passenger traffic by air is showing phenomenal growth. Air freight is mainly handled by a private company but the State internal airline has a virtual monopoly on the passenger side. State enterprise extends into road passenger transport with the Railways as the largest operator of coaches. Carriage of goods by road is, however, in the hands of a multiplicity of private operators, most of them small. Suburban passenger transport is mainly a municipal function and almost all such enterprises lose money in a desperate fight against the ubiquitous private car.

Communications of all types are handled by Government through the Post and Telegraph Office and the Broadcasting Corporation — an autonomous successor to the old Broadcasting Service (which was a Government Department) — although few people can detect any significant difference. The Broadcasting Corporation owns and operates commercial and non-commercial radio stations and one mixed television channel. Almost everyone possesses a radio and over 50 per cent of dwellings have a television set. Licence fees and advertising revenue enable the Corporation to operate profitably. A second television channel is likely now that nearly all of the country can receive signals from a chain of transmitters and repeaters, but this will probably also be State owned. The Broadcasting Corporation is frequently abused but the Post Office is rightly regarded as one of the most efficient enterprises in the country. It is also the largest with its postal, telegraphic, savings bank and numerous agency functions.

Almost all electricity generation is by the State which also operates the high tension grid system which covers both main islands, with an underwater direct-current cable as the link between them. Retail distribution is, however, a function of municipalities and *ad hoc* Power Boards. Electricity consumption per head is among the highest in the world as all but the most remote houses are reticulated and the cost of domestic power is relatively low.

Historically New Zealand has relied on water to generate electricity and this is still easily the most important source of electrical energy. The near exhaustion of sites for hydro-electric power stations in the North Island and the rapidly rising costs of developing new stations in the South Island is, however, leading to some diversification. Within recent years a large coal-fired thermal station, a geothermal power scheme and an oil-based generation plant have been developed. Currently, it is proposed to use natural gas from the Kapuni field to generate electricity until demand for the gas as such rises to economic levels. It is proposed to distribute the natural gas through the reticulation systems of existing coal-gas plants in some cities and towns but their equipment and distribution systems are antiquated with resulting high costs. Furthermore, consumers clearly prefer electricity for cooking and heating. An odd aspect of the natural gas proposals is that they envisage domestic demand only, whereas industrial use is necessary to secure a fully economic rate of gas offtake.

New Zealand is 'over-shopped' in comparison with other Western countries and this appears to be only partly explained by low density of population. Another factor may be the Kiwi's preference for self-employment wherever possible, even at a lower income per hour than

if he worked for wages. Certainly, this is the position of many small shopkeepers, especially 'dairy' proprietors. The corner dairy is New Zealand's closest equivalent to the American drug store, the only difference being that medicines, apart from aspirins and throat lozenges, are not handled. There is little evidence of a decline in the number of shops per thousand of population although increasingly severe competition from supermarkets is being experienced by grocers. Butchers who cut up their own meat still exist as always although it can only be a matter of time before they are superseded by supermarkets. Bakeries have, however, almost disappeared.

Although retailing shows little evidence of rationalisation, great changes have taken place in wholesale distribution. The traditional wholesale firms handling a wide range of products and maintaining travellers on the road as well as large warehouses are clearly on the way out. The usual reason advanced is import licensing but manufacturers would probably have adopted direct selling in any case. Wholesalers have not of course disappeared entirely but the squeeze is evidently on the middle man. Large inner-city department stores are also facing difficult trading because of traffic congestion and the fanning out of suburban dormitories. As in other activities, shops that are well managed do well, the rest do not.

New Zealand is perhaps the only country in the world where all major financial institutions are either Government owned or subject to overseas control. In the case of commercial banks, the largest is Government owned, the rest have head offices in London or Australia. Branch banking along British lines is practised; so there are only five such institutions. They obtain most of their funds from current account deposits that bear no interest but entitle the holders to full and cheap cheque facilities. Cheque usage is among the highest in the world; there is no giro system although it has been advocated. The banks do most of their lending on overdraft rather than fixed loans and the flexibility of the overdraft system is well suited to the needs of borrowers because of the marked seasonality of the economy. Commercial banks specialise in supplying working capital and their only serious competitors in this field are the stock and station agents who are the main lenders on short term to farmers.

The commercial banks also operate savings bank departments but here they face strong competition from local trustee savings banks and the nationwide savings bank services offered by the Post Office.

The Government requires a high proportion of all savings bank deposits to be invested in Government securities (100 per cent in the case of the Post Office Savings Bank). The trustee savings bank movement has shown great vitality in recent years and there are now banks in all major towns in the country. The appeal of these banks is very parochial and much is made of their local investment policy and distribution of profits to local worthy causes. The Government lays down uniform deposit interest rates for all savings banks.

Life assurance is very popular, encouraged in part by income tax concessions on premiums, and the building society movement has also great strength. New Zealanders are prone to gamble and it is not therefore surprising that the lottery type of 'terminating' building society has made much more rapid progress than other building societies which are akin to savings banks. Life assurance companies are heavy investors in Government and local authority securities, and traditionally also in dwellings. In recent years they have shown considerable interest in equity shares and 'sale-and-lease-back' arrangements on commercial buildings. The largest lender on long term is the State Advances Corporation which draws its funds from Government. The Corporation lends mainly to farmers and house builders with little capital, and its interest rates are low. It also administers the sizeable pool of State rental houses. New Zealand has the usual complement of finance companies and trustee investment companies, solicitors being also important sources of mortgage money.

Most lending in New Zealand is on mortgage, secured on property. Banks, however, prefer to secure their overdrafts on 'floating' debentures. In recent years many larger companies have borrowed directly from the public on debenture and share issues have also been popular. For industry, however, reinvested profits and depreciation allowances represent the main source of capital. Interest rates have hardened steadily since the war; long-term Government bonds now yield over 5 per cent, prime first mortgages 6 per cent, finance company commercial loans over 10 per cent and consumer hire purchase loans over 15 per cent.

In July 1967 New Zealand changed over to decimal currency. The new unit is the dollar, equal to half a pound or ten shillings. The dollar is divided into one hundred cents. A great fuss broke out some time ago over designs for the new decimal coins which were indeed undistinguished. A popular victory ensued with the Government withdrawing the original designs and substituting fresh ones which were judged more acceptable. The designs of the new bank notes have, however, been well received. They feature the Queen on the front and native birds on the back, the whole having a pleasing balance of dignity and simplicity.

New Zealand's traditional pro-British sentiments took a further knock with the decision to replace the pound with the dollar but the implicit veering of sentiment towards the United States (of necessity rather than of choice) is a fair reflection of the national mood.

In common with other Western countries, New Zealand has seen rapid expansion of service activities of all sorts since the war. Today domestic and personal services, including the small number of armed forces, comprise only a quarter of the total. Full-time domestic servants in private employ have virtually disappeared and hotels, clubs, etc., face great difficulty in attracting enough labour. In fact without the help of people on working holidays from Australia, mainly girls, New Zealand would have no high-grade travel accommodation at all, especially in remote tourist resorts.

Administrative and professional services are expanding very rapidly although Government and local authorities are not appreciably increasing their proportionate demand on the labour force. The concentration of Central Government and head office administrative functions in the capital has made Wellington a city of clerks and administrators. Not surprisingly the shortage of typists is most acute in Wellington. Another facet of centralised administration is the large amount of office space occupied by Government in the capital and to a lesser extent in other main centres. Traditionally Government has not paid rates on its administrative and social service buildings but the regional inequity of this has now been partially recognised and Government makes a greater contribution to local authority revenue.

Females outnumber males in both major sub-divisions of the services sector and the growth of services owes much to the rapidly rising female participation in the work force. In the last few years the annual increase in the number of women workers has been roughly double that for males but the less buoyant economic conditions likely in the next few years may see a marked change. Equal pay for men and women was enacted for the State services some years ago and its effects are slowly penetrating the economy as a whole.

Government in New Zealand is ubiquitous and most people seem to like it this way so long as they can vote out of office both Central Government and local authorities every three years if they are not satisfied with their performance. There is no constitution, so Parliament is sovereign; today the office of Governor-General has no political significance. Parliament currently comprises 80 representatives of the people, 76 from European electorates of roughly equal size (in terms of population but not of course of area) and four from Maori electorates. Polling is on the 'first-past-the-post' system which makes it very difficult for candidates outside the main political parties to be elected. At the present time there are 44 members of the House of Representatives belonging to the National Party, 35 Labour members and one Social Crediter. The general election at the end of 1966 saw an 87 per cent turn-out of electors (it is compulsory to register one's name on the electoral roll but not to vote), National obtaining 43 per cent of the total vote, Labour 41 per cent and Social Credit 14 per cent. These parties each contested all seats. At every election a few independents make a hopeless effort to get elected and the votes recorded for the odd Communist candidate are derisory.

New Zealanders appear to have fairly stable preferences for one or other of the two main parties although on most issues their policies are hardly distinguishable and their actions when in power even more like those of Tweedledum and Tweedledee. Both span a wide political spectrum with an overlap that is nearly as great. The Labour Party's centre of gravity is of course further to the left than National's but a good proportion of parliamentarians would be equally happy in either. Social Credit, the Johnny-come-lately, owes much of its support to the common 'a plague on both your houses' attitude but to the extent that it has a political philosophy, apart from funny money, it is more right-wing than the National Party. Thus on the Vietnam issue, Social Credit sees eye to eye with the Government. The Labour Party and the National Party are both conservative in the narrow sense, all radical fires having been long since doused, and in this they faithfully reflect the community's aversion to change even when it is unavoidable.

The Labour Party's main strength is in the larger urban areas, where it holds most of the seats, and in the Maori electorates, whereas National holds all farming seats (except that won by Social Credit in 1966) and the blue-chip urban electorates. The parties share the provincial cities. As a smaller and smaller proportion of the electorate can remember the depression, the Labour Party's basic appeal would appear to be diminishing and it is having difficulty in finding a new image. The evident influence of the industrial labour movement with its restrictionist philosophy makes it difficult for the parliamentary party to pose as apostles of progress. In recent years the National Party has not succeeded in identifying itself with anything in particular, certainly not private enterprise, which was once its credo.

The relative importance of Prime Minister, Cabinet and parliamentary caucus naturally depends on the personalities of the people concerned. As the business of administration has become more exacting, an inner Cabinet with special responsibility for economic matters has come into being informally. Behind this lies the Treasury which has very great influence, as in most countries. The Public Service in New Zealand is traditionally non-political and there are special devices to prevent political sympathies influencing promotion at all levels. No one would dispute the desirability of these for the lower grades of public servants but they sometimes result in senior appointments going to men with strong ideological convictions contrary to the policy of Government. This is not conducive to good administration or implementation of Government policy and in recent years tension between the Public Service and Government has been engendered by the overt opposition of the Public Service Association to the Government's policies.

Departments of State are administered by Permanent Heads responsible to the corresponding Cabinet Ministers. Treasury is the co-ordinating agency on the financial side and the State Services Commission on the administrative side. Departmental reports are tabled in the House of Representatives but Parliament as distinct from Government has no effective control over Departments. Still less has it any effective control over Government trading agencies, especially those organised as Corporations, such as the Reserve Bank, Bank of New Zealand, Air New Zealand, National Airways Corporation, State Insurance Office, Government Life Office, State Advances Corporation and Broadcasting Corporation. This list incidentally gives some idea of the range of Government trading activities; to it must be added, of course, the Railways, the Post Office, the Electricity Department, and the State Coal Mines, not to mention substantial financial interest in the Tasman Pulp and Paper Company and the New Zealand Steel Company. Public servants in New

Zealand have been historically ill paid but they enjoy a heavily subsidised pension scheme. The service is also very jealous of recruitment
from the outside – a defensive reaction not untypical of the country
but more serious in this instance than in most because of the unusual
importance of Government in New Zealand.

Chapter 7

The Contemporary Economic Scene

A T THE TIME OF writing (early 1967) the dominant economic issue in New Zealand is the balance of payments, as it has so often been in the past. Most foreign exchange crises have been occasioned by a slump in export prices and this element is present today. Wool, which last season realised nearly 42 pence a pound for a record clip and thereby netted the country almost £120 million of foreign exchange, will average under 37 pence a pound this season. What is nearly as bad, the Wool Commission, which set its floor price for the season at 36 pence a pound, is likely to wind up purchasing over a third of the clip so that foreign exchange receipts for wool will be under £90 million. Had the Commission not intervened, the price might well have dropped as low as 30 pence a pound.

The drop in wool prices, unexpected as it was, is by no means the only reason for the serious balance of payments situation although the Government is naturally using it as the excuse for its troubles. The main culprit is a national spending spree that began four years ago with Government, local authorities and the private sector all contributing to an unparalleled upsurge in spending, especially capital expenditure. Export receipts in this period have risen substantially but not enough to meet the soaring bill for imports and other overseas expenditure. The fall in wool receipts has only advanced the day of reckoning. The balance of payments deficit for 1966–67 is over £100 million but it was already £93 million in the previous year when wool receipts were at a record level. Until the last few months the Government had taken no effective action to avert a crisis.

There is little point in recounting in detail the events leading up to the present situation. On the other hand, an understanding of the main elements of post-war economic affairs is necessary to appreciate the measures required to restore external balance. Overseas receipts and payments must somehow be equated, at least approximately, because New Zealand has almost exhausted its borrowing capacity abroad. What remains to be seen is whether this can be accomplished without sacrificing full employment, rightly regarded as a major achievement of the post-war period. If full employment can be preserved, the quest for external balance may still have damaging implications for longer-run economic growth. The country's growth prospects of course depend on the availability and prosperity of export markets as well as on internal policy decisions but overseas market prospects will be canvassed later.

At the beginning of 1950, just prior to the Korean Wool Boom, New Zealand's external balance sheet was healthy and foreign exchange reserves were quite adequate. (The exchange rate was again at parity with Sterling following the 1948 appreciation.) Then came a surge in export receipts, followed almost immediately by an even greater surge in import and other overseas payments, which wiped out the reserves accumulated in the previous year. This sort of pattern has subsequently become commonplace and for brevity it is depicted graphically in Diagram A.

The remarkable constancy, about a strongly rising trend, exhibited by export receipts is notable. Import payments and net overseas payments for services (invisibles) together have fluctuated much more than export receipts, despite the continuous use of import and exchange controls – ostensibly to maintain balance of payments equilibrium. Paradoxically, exports over which New Zealand has virtually no influence in the short run have displayed greater stability than imports which economic policy is supposed to control. Balance of payments instability has originated within the country rather than abroad. Underlying these fluctuations there has evidently been a trend deterioration, due to the failure of invisible receipts to increase as rapidly as invisible payments as well as to excessive growth of both visible and invisible payments abroad.

There is naturally no simple explanation for the marked worsening of the balance of payments position in the sixties. Certainly, the terms of trade cannot be blamed although they fluctuated considerably over the years. One has to look to spending within the country for the proximate cause of increasing external imbalance. Diagram B portrays the key series: consumer spending, public authority expenditure and private capital formation. To facilitate comparison these are plotted on ratio scales so that equal slopes indicate equal rates of growth. A 5 per cent per annum reference line is also shown for each type of spending, based on 2 per cent

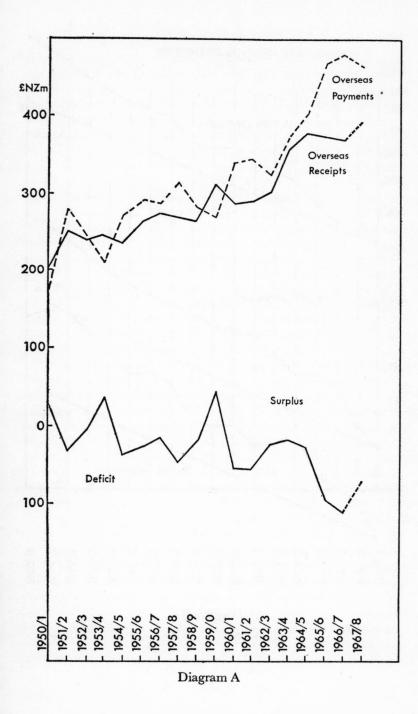

Diagram A

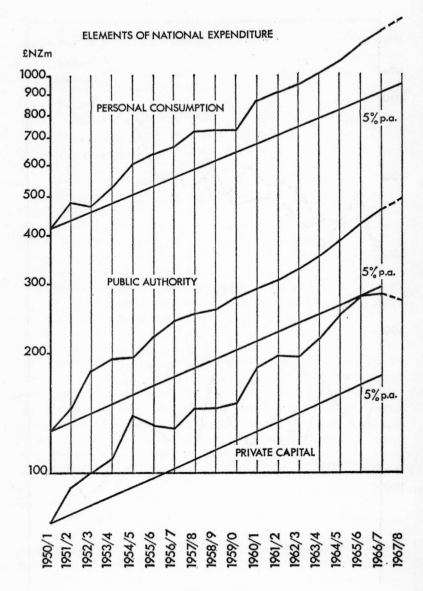

ELEMENTS OF NATIONAL EXPENDITURE

£NZm

1000
900
800 — PERSONAL CONSUMPTION
700
600
500
400

300 — PUBLIC AUTHORITY

200

PRIVATE CAPITAL

100

5% p.a.

5% p.a.

5% p.a.

1950/1 1951/2 1952/3 1953/4 1954/5 1955/6 1956/7 1957/8 1958/9 1959/0 1960/1 1961/2 1962/3 1963/4 1964/5 1965/6 1966/7 1967/8

Diagram B

labour force growth, 2 per cent productivity increase and an allowance of 1 per cent for price inflation. Rises in expenditure of this order would have been consistent with New Zealand's long run economic performance in the post-war period, but spending has rarely shown such modest but realistic increases. A 1 per cent allowance for price inflation is justified because world prices have shown a rising trend of approximately this order over the period as a whole.

The ease with which the country has until now been able to borrow abroad has delayed the inevitable cut-back in spending. The deflationary measures taken in 1958 and 1961 were relaxed too soon and rises in export receipts in the years following sparked off new inflationary bursts. The interaction of overseas receipts, internal incomes and expenditure and overseas payments is masked to some extent by fluctuations in stocks of imported goods and by changes in import licensing allocations. The latter are largely ignored here because import licensing has proved impotent as a balance of payments regulator although it is effective as a protective device.

Policy measures are slow to act and the data informing policy slow to collect but the fundamental reason for the failure of economic regulation in the sixties has been the unwillingness of the (National) Government to take any action that might weaken its chances at the next hustings on the widely accepted premise that the 1958 Budget was responsible for Labour's subsequent electoral defeat in 1960. It is at least arguable, however, that Labour's downfall was due rather to the glaring incongruity between a deflationary Budget and the extravagant election promises made less than a year earlier, promises which contributed to the necessity for deflation. The 1958 Budget and the automatic deflationary effect of a fall in farm incomes, stemming from declines in butter, cheese and wool prices, restored external balance, at least momentarily, and also balanced supply and demand internally without generating substantial unemployment. Unfortunately for the (Labour) Government, few people liked a balanced economy after years of near-boom conditions. The endemic 'eat-your-cake-and-have-it' disease became epidemic with the Opposition as the main carriers. Inertia apart, the main reason for the present Government's failure to take effective deflationary action in 1966 was the inability of the National Party to swallow its earlier words. The Prime Minister's dictum 'steady does it' may well outlive him and the damage to the economy resulting from inaction, but an importunate electorate must share the blame.

A new element in the formulation of economic policy is the Monetary and Economic Council, set up in 1961 to advise Government and given the right to publish its views. In the event the Council has proved something of a thorn in the Government's flesh because it has been generally highly critical of policy or lack of policy in the face of the deteriorating balance of payments situation. The Government would probably like to bury the Council quietly if it could and the Labour Party has said that it will do so when next in power. On immigration, however, the Council has roundly supported the Government's policy of not encouraging heavy immigration, especially of assisted immigrants. In current affairs of course the Council, composed of accountants and economists, and with a small expert staff, pleases practically no one because it has argued strongly for disinflation – never a popular remedy for a superficially attractive ill.

New Zealand in early 1967 is faced with the necessity of sharply reducing its overseas trading deficit, preferably in a way that avoids significant unemployment in the short run and minimises the check to long-run growth. The Government recognises that this calls for deflationary fiscal measures as well as more stringent import licensing. Restrictive monetary policies have been in force for some time and have demonstrated their inadequacy without supporting fiscal measures. Import licences for the 1966–67 (June) year were reduced appreciably a year ago and allocations for the 1967–68 year are being cut further, but except in a few cases, such as motor-cars, their role is supportive rather than directive. A weakness of import licensing, as it applies to raw materials and semi-finished goods for further processing, is that manufacturers, faced with buoyant demand for their products, are in a very strong position to blackmail the Government into issuing supplementary licences. Unemployment is still a potent bogy, although it is weakening all the time as the proportion of people who can remember any, grows steadily smaller. In the case of capital equipment, there is more scope for licensing cuts but again better results are likely to ensue if producers decide their requirements for imported plant and machinery in the light of potential demand rather than availability of import licences, the issue of which must always be largely arbitrary. After thirty years of the system, there are few 'inessential' consumer goods imports left to be squeezed.

Two years ago when overseas reserves were thought to be reasonably satisfactory, the Government courageously decided to exempt completely a wide range of goods from import licensing. Most of these were essentials, such as fuels, but many textiles were included. Courage was required then because almost everyone, except consumers and farmers, likes import licensing despite frequent ritual noises to the contrary. Producers of competing products naturally like import controls, as do the workers they employ, but so do importers generally because they are protected against newcomers and scarce licences command a premium. Even more courage is now being required of the Government to withstand pressures to re-impose licensing on exempt items. One of the pressure groups is the ultra right-wing Constitutional Society which is currently displaying as little aptitude for economics as it has for politics in the past. So far the Government has stood firm and indeed indicated that the complete dismantling of import licensing will be proceeded with as soon as possible. This has always been one of the National Party's policy planks but it would appear to enjoy higher priority now than previously. Presumably the business wing of the party is somewhat less influential than usual. The Labour Party has of course always been strongly protectionist. Another straw in the wind is the decision to discontinue the 'no-remittance' licence scheme whereby New Zealanders possessing overseas funds could, in a wide variety of circumstances, use them to import goods – notably motor-cars. Although the arrangement worked well initially, it has naturally discouraged anyone acquiring funds overseas from remitting them home and has thereby contributed to the balance of payments crisis.

As the first instalment of its deflationary package, the Government in February 1967 announced a virtual stand-still of its own expenditure and, by temporarily abolishing the interest rate premium on local authority borrowing, it ensured that public authority expenditure as a whole would show little increase in 1967–68. After a rise of no less than 9 per cent in the preceding year, this of itself will have a marked stabilising effect. Consumer subsidies on butter, flour and bread were discontinued as part of the expenditure freeze and this gave rise to some ill-informed criticism. The most interesting aspect was the fact that the President of the Federation of Labour led the attack and not the leader of the Parliamentary Labour Party. An amusing example of the humourlessness of many protesters is afforded by the unfortunate initials 'CARP' of the Campaign Against Rising Prices, a group of women pledged to fight price increases, which came into being as a result of the removal of subsidies. Milk, eggs and gas are still subsidised but the annual bill for these is only a fraction of that for butter, flour and bread. No significant change in butter consumption is likely but wheat imports may well fall appreciably as bread was formerly so cheap that it was not worthwhile avoiding waste.

When Parliament reassembled in April taxation increases were implemented on such things as motor-cars, petrol, spirits and tobacco. These will complement increases already announced in Post Office, railways and electricity charges. Higher taxes on 'luxuries' will undoubtedly improve the political acceptability of deflation but the more important question is whether they will be adequate to forestall external insolvency. The Government is evidently relying also on other deflationary influences currently at work.

The most important of these is the decay of the investment boom which has occurred with little assistance from Government but doubtless influenced by the general climate of uncertainty about the country's immediate economic future. There are also signs that consumer expenditure is being checked for the same reason. Another factor favourable to a sharp reduction in internal and external spending is the currently high level of stocks. A further deflationary measure that appears certain in 1967 is a reduction in the 'guaranteed' price for butterfat, on top of the lower prices currently being received for wool and lamb. Under the Act establishing the Dairy Prices Authority, yet another statutory body, the basic price for butterfat used in butter and cheese manufacture can be reduced by at most 5 per cent in a season. The Dairy Industry is in a weak bargaining position as its account with the Reserve Bank is in deficit, yet dairy farmers are receiving the full price realised for by-products. The Government is, however, concerned that farmers generally do not cut back development expenditure and fertiliser application too sharply, otherwise exports may suffer.

This raises the question of New Zealand's export prospects. In the short run some recovery in the wool market appears likely, but the Wool Commission will almost certainly be forced to lower its support price. It is too early to judge whether the 1966–67 recession is mainly due to destocking by mills and intermediaries or to a secular decline in the demand for coarse wool but the former is undoubtedly a major factor. There is a possibility of course that buyers are taking advantage of the high support price to force the Wool Commission to carry stocks which otherwise they would have to hold. In the case of butter, the short-run prospects are for a further easing of price following the recent increase in United Kingdom quotas and, with the greatly enlarged New Zealand exports of lamb to the United Kingdom, some further decline in lamb price is likely. Overall, the prospects are for more or less stable export prices in the next year or so.

Looking further ahead the crystal ball is much less clear. If the United Kingdom application to enter the European Economic Community is unsuccessful, there is no reason to expect dramatic changes in sales of lamb and dairy products but the slow growth of the British market will inexorably force prices down unless additional supplies can be diverted elsewhere. For these commodities development of new markets at satisfactory prices will inevitably be slow and production changes in the direction of lower fat content in milk and later slaughtering of lambs may well be necessary. Demand for mutton is more elastic than demand for lamb and New Zealand lambs are too fat for most markets. If the United Kingdom is successful in joining the Common Market, these problems will be faced sooner rather than later, although no doubt some interim arrangements will be made to reduce the immediate impact on New Zealand of British entry into the European Economic Community. As regards wool, everything depends on the true state of demand but prices in excess of 36 pence a pound would appear unlikely on any reckoning. Modification of the present auction system to facilitate further processing and direct sales to mills may do something to minimise the consequences of permanently lower prices.

Turning to forest products, the key issue is the extent to which Australia is prepared to allow sales of linerboard from New Zealand against the opposition of a major indigenous producer or whether she will invoke an escape clause in the Limited Free Trade Agreement. There are undoubtedly benefits to both countries in a rationalisation of forest utilisation but reason is seldom the sole determinant of economic policy. The sensible thing would clearly be for New Zealand to specialise in the manufacture of pulp, newsprint and linerboard for the local market and for export, mainly to Australia, and to import from Australia paper products for which local demand is too small to permit efficient production. Unfortunately, there are interests in both countries geared to supplying a protected local market with almost a full range of products. Goodwill on both sides and a minimum of xenophobia will clearly be required to secure joint exploitation of forest resources to the maximum benefit of both Australia and New Zealand.

Tourism, which today is a minor foreign exchange earner, could be expanded quite rapidly given the will to do so but a curious ambivalence on this issue is evident at all levels. This is explored in a later chapter; for the present only the economics of tourism are relevant. In the euphoric days of 1963 when the Agricultural Development Conference was convened, the prospects for New Zealand's traditional exports appeared rather more assured than at present and the claims of tourism tended to be downgraded, in effect if not in intent. The 100 per cent export content of tourism and the relatively low import content of facilities for overseas visitors, however, make the industry deserving of more attention than it has received in the past. Its structure is a little unfortunate; the (Government) Tourist Hotel Corporation, which operates a string of high quality hotels in the various tourist destinations, makes handsome losses because of high labour costs and under-utilisation of capacity, whereas profits of private enterprise from tourism are not widely known. This has discouraged investment in the industry but Government assistance for approved projects has to some extent offset the dearth of private investment capital. The tourist industry would of course benefit greatly from devaluation of the New Zealand pound, especially as high-class accommodation is fully priced by world standards and travel to New Zealand (except from Australia) is expensive.

The general issue of devaluation is naturally canvassed every time the country experiences a balance of payments crisis and the present occasion is no exception. In principle, some such general means of encouraging exports and discouraging imports has much to commend it, but the timing is evidently critical. In any country devaluation is more likely to achieve the desired switch of resources when economic conditions are relatively depressed and this is especially true of New Zealand because of the Arbitration Court's general wage order system and the widespread cost-plus attitude of businessmen. On this score the middle of 1968 (middle of year because it is the seasonal low point of the economy) might well be an appropriate time for devaluation. So far as terms of trade are concerned, however, the case is not strong, although there are technical reasons for thinking that import prices have risen more in the last decade than the official index suggests. The main argument against devaluation is simply that the economy today is too buoyant to prevent local costs and prices rising to nearly the same extent and thereby defeating the purpose of the exercise.

The current economic issue boils down to the containment of demand pressures as a prerequisite for identifying the structural changes necessary in the next few years. Whether fundamental changes, such as devaluation, are necessary at all can only be determined after a sustained period of comparative deflation but more immediately the need is to reduce usage of imported materials by cutting down on overtime and generally restricting employment more closely to the regular labour force. In recent years the labour market has been so stretched that large numbers of married women and superannuitants have been able to find work. Part-time employment and the holding of second jobs is also common. Associated with the extreme ease of securing employment there has not surprisingly been a very high rate of labour turnover and casual absenteeism which have pushed up costs and limited production. With workers in such a strong bargaining position, wage rates as determined by individual awards have risen substantially and above-award margins even more so. Unions have been displaying greater interest in award negotiations as their confidence in the general wage order system has declined. General wage orders affect minimum award rates of pay throughout the economy but the periodic hearings have appeared increasingly irrelevant as above-award margins have become bigger and more common.

A more realistic level of economic activity will not of course cause above-award margins to disappear, as they reflect regional differences in demand for labour as well as differences in skill and energy, but a closer correspondence between legal minima and actual rewards is desirable. A better balance between supply and demand within the country will also induce greater attention to costs and profits by management which has had an easy time in the post-war period. Only in labour relations have employers had real difficulty and even then the market for products was so buoyant that it was all too easy to pay higher wages or allow unnecessary overtime, passing on the resulting higher costs to consumers. The economy badly needs a period of tighter trading conditions to make a dent in the cost-plus attitude of firms producing mainly for the home market. A rash of bankruptcies will be an early result but these will only be the firms which, overseas, would never have been started or would have failed much sooner. Inefficient businesses enjoy a padded economy just as much as workers; the only difference is that they derive even more financial advantage.

Whatever the precise mode of adjustment, the New Zealand economy is beginning a period of less easy trading conditions, internally as well as externally. If the traditional defensive reaction prevails the long term consequences could be severe. If on the other hand restrictive practices and easygoing arrangements are sacrificed, the economy will emerge far stronger. The concept of the Welfare State as it applies to individuals who through no fault of their own fall on hard times need not be weakened at all – the country being well able to afford generous welfare provisions for those in need. But the common extension of the Welfare State to prop up inefficient firms, backward sectors of the economy and entrenched interests of all sorts must go, or there is no hope. The great weakness of import licensing is that it does buttress up the business *status quo* irrespective of current performance. New Zealand has in the past been saved from its natural inclination towards a thoroughgoing extension of 'cost-plus' by the impossibility of extending this to the export sector, but the temptation has always been there. In fact the original guaranteed price concept for dairying envisaged a complete divorce between internal pay-outs and overseas realisations – although how anyone imagined this succeeding with a fixed exchange rate is now hard to see. In the event, Kiwi pragmatism saved the day. Dairy farmers, once they had recovered from their sense of betrayal, got to work and increased productivity to the extent that an 'economic dairy unit' (one man) is now about three times the size it was when the guaranteed price scheme was introduced. Currently, efforts are being made to prop up apple growing in much the same way but this will not last long.

The economy will no doubt continue to expand, new industries will be established and old ones will grow, but clearly more attention must be paid to efficiency and profitability. In the economic sense efficiency and profitability are the same thing but in a country abounding with controls and regulations, and prone to private restrictive agreements, a wide difference can exist. Where licensing arrangements of any sort are involved profitability gives little guide to efficiency in the technical sense, much less to efficiency in the economic sense. In manufacturing this is especially true as many industries established in the last twenty years have been designed to protect markets, often with the knowledge that production would be on too small a scale to be fully profitable. Very little attention has been given so far to the exploitation of the resources New Zealand has in abundance – which are not very numerous. Farming, forestry and electricity are notable exceptions; apart from plenty of land and a temperate, moist climate the only major resource which offers New Zealand any comparative advantage over other countries is a well-educated and adaptable work force. In some activities, such as light engineering, this is appreciated but too often the mistake has been made of setting up consumer goods industries needing large production to hold down costs. This is commonly associated with gross under-utilization of plant and equipment because of the labour shortage or restrictions upon hours of work. There is abundant scope for more efficient production and distribution as well as for new lines of economic endeavour, both of which will ensure a continued rise in living standards; but New Zealand has tried the experiment of an over-guided and over-padded economy which has not worked. It remains to be seen whether current difficulties are sufficient to induce the right sort and degree of radicalism.

Chapter 8

Culture

THE DEVELOPMENT of New Zealand's culture has been hesitant and wary. For one thing, the early settlers and their immediate descendants were too busy with the fundamentals of existence to be much concerned about the arts. New Zealand was primarily a country on the make and its inhabitants were content for the most part to concern themselves with mundane matters. They lived very much in the present and for the present. Those settlers who were interested in ideas, in art, in literature or in music found themselves living perforce in two worlds. Charlotte Brontë's friend, Mary Taylor, presented the dilemma very plainly in a letter written from Wellington in 1848. 'I can hardly explain to you the queer feeling of living, as I do, in two places at once. One world containing books, England and all the people with whom I can exchange an idea; the other all that I can actually hear and see and speak to. The separation is as complete as between the things in a picture and the things in a room . . .' New Zealand artists of every kind spent nearly a century struggling to bring together the things of the picture and the things of the room. The struggle was a desperate one; when poets wrote about New Zealand, they used the stylised English diction which was all that they knew, but reality fled before their very words; painters depicted New Zealand scenery in terms of the dim Romanticism in vogue in Europe, and the bush, the mountains and the rivers faded into genteel backdrops; novelists worked away diligently at Maori material, reducing the race to the heroic, primitive savage of Victorian melodrama. The story of New Zealand culture lies in the hesitant steps of its artists towards the creative expression of a New Zealand as opposed to an English reality. Slowly writers and painters saw the falsity of their work, but while the whole European community looked to England and 'home', even after fifty or sixty years of life in New Zealand, it was impossible to do more than balance on the edge of the picture frame, unhappily measuring the distance down into the room itself. New Zealand remained closely linked with Britain, not only because of the market it offered for primary produce, but also because people in New Zealand wished it so. A sense of nationhood only began to appear during the First World War, when a community spirit was, as it were, thrust upon New Zealanders to distinguish them as a people from the English or the Scottish. This new feeling of community gave some help to struggling artists, more and more conscious of the schizophrenic nature of their position, and the 1930's saw a determined, if self-conscious, effort to close the gap between the picture and the room. Writers, painters and musicians wished to express New Zealand as they really saw it, not as it appeared when strained through the accumulated paraphernalia of another culture. That they succeeded is a tribute to their purpose and integrity. They were able to express the New Zealand idiom by deliberately putting aside the English cultural vision, but the cost of the effort is revealed in the fumbling, self-conscious writing and the odd backward glance to the cosy warmth of the picture. The depression and Second World War came as traumatic experiences which finally jolted New Zealand society into adult nationhood. Artists of today live very much in the reality of the room, suffering its discomforts and accepting its pleasures with a nonchalance born of long acquaintance. New Zealand is now experiencing its first burst of unforced, creative activity embracing all fields of cultural endeavour.

The hesitancies and struggles of New Zealand culture have been most fully expressed in its literature. Many of the educated settlers brought with them the English tradition of competent versifying, but it was many years before more gifted poets appeared. For at least seventy years indifferent poets cheerfully described the glories of life in New Zealand, although always from the safety of the picture scene. A versifier had only to put pen to paper for the whole apparatus of English poetry to appear – dryads, gods, poetic diction – transforming his subject-matter into yet another lyric or epic in the high Romantic tradition with heavy overtones of Wordsworth. The depression of the 1880's and '90's stirred up a social conscience among most thinking New Zealanders and would-be poets devoted themselves to public, optimistic verse (New Zealand's national hymn[1] dates from this period) or else indulged in sentimental, nostalgic rhymes, varied at times by heavy-handed ballads in what was considered 'the colonial tradition'. In fact, poetry remained of little account until the late 1920's.

[1] 'God Defend New Zealand' by Thomas Bracken, 1878.

The early novelists struggled much harder towards the expression of New Zealand reality. Many of them were accurate and interested observers of the country, and tried to incorporate the Maori material which lay so close to hand. Sir George Grey's collection of Polynesian myths and legends had stimulated great interest in the Maori as a noble savage, and had opened up the great treasure house of Maori mythology. Most novels exploiting Maori material and the exigencies of colonial life, where anything could and did happen, degenerate quickly into improbable melodramas, full of stock characters and loaded with local colour which had to be explained to the English audience in the form of sermons, lecturettes or highly instructive conversations between characters. Some novelists used the recording technique, with an immigrant family as a device to introduce at least some story into the flood of facts. Often the story ran away with itself and the facts being recorded were themselves frequently awry. Of the early novelists, only two are of any account whatever; William Satchell succeeded in unobtrusively describing the flavour of New Zealand life, but he was only too conscious of the need to join up the elements of the picture and the room. In *The Greenstone Door*[1] he went back to the beginning and by using an historical perspective tried to reconstruct the past to give meaning to the present. The other writer was Jane Mander (1877–1949) whose *The Story of a New Zealand River*[2] discusses the problems of women in a setting of the Northland gumfields. The story is built around personal relationships, one of which describes the clash between the pioneer active husband and the well-educated, refined wife, a clash reflected in all New Zealand life, where, as Samuel Butler remarked, 'It does not do to speak of . . . Bach's fugues.'

The philistinism of New Zealand society was a stultifying, depressing influence on any promising artist. It was little wonder that Katherine Mansfield (1888–1923), the greatest writer New Zealand has yet produced, retreated into the picture world completely, unable to bear the division between actual reality and cultural reality. A later novelist wrote of the problem: 'You were English and not English . . . you were brought up on blue-bells and primroses and daffodils and robins in the snow . . . one day you realised there were no robins and no snow and you felt cheated.' There was a desperate feeling of 'hanging on with one hand, and the other full of seas'. Katherine Mansfield left New Zealand permanently in 1909 at the

[1] 1914.   [2] Begun 1900, published 1920.

age of twenty-one to become a major writer in the short-story form in the stimulating climate of English contemporary literature. Her greatest achievement lies in those stories which re-create with an exacting insight New Zealand life as she had experienced it; she was the first writer to use New Zealand material naturally in the European tradition. Although she was forced to run away from New Zealand, Katherine Mansfield, like most creative expatriates, remained fascinated by her memories of it; perhaps the perspective necessary to give life in New Zealand its own unexaggerated shape could only be provided by a 12,000-mile flight.

Between the two wars came the determined achievement of a whole group of novelists, poets and short-story writers. That they were still troubled by the cultural dilemma is quite evident, but their writing shows a deliberate attempt to explore and express their exact position as New Zealanders. M. H. Holcroft, an essayist of considerable perception, assisted the struggle by charting the course taken by New Zealand letters to the present time, carefully marking the hazards which seemed most dangerous. The most obvious trouble was the lack of a mythology, a common ground which provided a reason for the kind of life New Zealanders were living and creating and which could be presumed in any literary expression. English poetic tradition drew heavily on Greek and Latin myths – obviously wrong for New Zealand – and Maori myths were not a common inheritance. The poets set out to provide their own myths, but these had the disadvantage of being individual creations and much of their emotive impact was lost upon the individual reader. James K. Baxter took advantage of the myth which adults make from childhood memories; time and again his poetry returns to this as a firm foundation from which it can make further exploratory sallies. His poetry has been read more widely than that of any other poet because the flavour of a New Zealand childhood is common experience to all New Zealanders.

Another great problem involved a sense of isolation from the rest of the creative world, together with a feeling of being stranded helpless on an alien shore. Both these sensations are best expressed in R. A. K. Mason's 'Sonnet on Brotherhood', where he speaks of:

> ... these beleaguered victims this our race
> betrayed alike by Fate's gigantic plot
> here in this far pitched perilous hostile place

this solitary hard-assaulted spot
fixed at the friendless outer edge of space.

As the poets struggled with their consciousness of themselves as New
Zealanders, trying to express their own doubts and uncertainties as
well as their social concern for the ordinary man caught in the trap
of the great depression, they were driven into a self-conscious attitude
which detracted considerably from the power of their verse. However, they were the first poets to write with any degree of technical
competence on the stuff of New Zealand life and to do it without
the artificialities of the picture on the wall. What was written in the
1930's laid the foundation for all future writing; no mean achievement by any standards, especially when the writers concerned were
perpetually frustrated by a lack of sympathy and appreciation among
the reading public of the country. The ordinary New Zealander
appeared quite indifferent to the culture which would one day be
his, and the poets were irritated to find themselves bound to a mundane, practical, pragmatic society. W. H. Oliver wrote in his poem
'The Remonstrance of the Norm':

Sir, save your temper,
I am your heart-break . . .
. . .
I am your birth and your
Death and your heart-beat.

Very little in the way of novels appeared until 1938 when Robin
Hyde published her book *The Godwits Fly*, attempting to express
the frustration of the cultural situation before which Katherine
Mansfield had fled to England. In 1939 John Mulgan published
Man Alone. He took the Hemingway character of a man alone and
sent him to New Zealand to live out his Hemingway loneliness in
the New Zealand environment. Mulgan achieved an unstrained
expression of the New Zealand scene and brilliantly caught the flat,
peculiarly laconic, speech used throughout the country. He also
recognised that his 'man alone' was closely allied to the state of
mind of New Zealand society – independent, self-reliant but unsure
of its direction.

A body of prose was slowly being written to support both these
authors. Many competent short-story writers were emerging, the
greatest of these probably being Frank Sargeson who also wrote
about the foot-loose man. The lone man has played a large part in

New Zealand's development. Surveyors, prospectors, high-country shepherds, forest rangers, odd-jobbing swagmen are the only eccentrics New Zealanders acknowledge with ease; Mulgan and Sargeson wrote about an immediately recognisable part of the national life.

The years following the Second World War have produced a complete transformation in the literary scene both in the outlook of writers and in the receptivity of the public. There has been a tremendous increase in the number of workmanlike novels, based immediately after the war on wartime experiences, but quickly making use of peacetime domestic situations – many of these novels were written by women and depended upon farce-like plots to maintain interest. Another group of writers concentrated on the problem of the Maori in modern life, the most exciting experiment being Sylvia Ashton-Warner's *Spinster*. The author draws upon her experiences as an infant mistress in a Maori school; she gives lightning sketches of the small children shadowed by the vague threat of life in the pakeha community.

There have also been many novels of urban life. Perhaps the finest is Janet Frame's *Owls Do Cry*, a story of family relationships in a small New Zealand town. The author has achieved what Robin Hyde so desperately longed to do – to describe human life in New Zealand as if it could be happening in any part of the world. The careful detail of the town immediately fixes the action in New Zealand, but this is done almost in passing as the author concentrates upon her family and its vulnerability to other humans. Novel reading in New Zealand seems unfortunately devoted to the game of spot-the-place in stories with a New Zealand background; readers like to recognise not only the shops and streets but even the people, and providing this sort of photographic detail has inhibited some urban novelists from reaching their best work. In common with the rest of the world, New Zealand has its writers of the dreary perverted fringe of the urban community. No work of real interest has been written in this vein, but Frank Sargeson's novel *Memoirs of a Peon*[1] is a robust picaresque tale parodying over-solemn short stories and novels devoted to middle-class sexual indiscretions. The story of a local Casanova is a new departure for New Zealand literature and it will be interesting to see where this injection of wit and spice will lead the novel next.

A considerable amount of heavy humour has been written about

[1] 1966.

New Zealand, most of it concerned with stereotyped, belly-bulging Maoris with a half-gallon flagon of beer and a kit full of pipis, or the equally stereotyped practical farmer, bluff, hearty and coarse, the epitome of 'the good keen man'. Very little subtle humour appears in New Zealand literature except in the short stories of Sargeson or of Maurice Duggan, the latter perhaps the most accomplished writer in this medium since the war.

Post-war poetry is quite different from that of the thirties, although it owes much to the hard work and integrity of the earlier poets. James K. Baxter is the only effective link between the two groups, and this mostly because he himself has never fitted into any pattern but has continued to write vigorous poetry exploring his own development. The poets of the fifties and sixties do not feel themselves battering against a monumental indifference on the part of society; people are much more ready to read poetry, to discuss it, even to buy it. The younger poets have no qualms about the spectre of the picture; indeed, they are so busy living in the room that the old ornament is barely spared a glance. It is still there of course, and will remain there, for New Zealand culture, when all is said and done, is primarily an Anglo-Saxon one, but today's poets do not feel threatened, isolated or alien because they live in New Zealand. Their poetry is the most individualistic, cosmopolitan work New Zealand has yet seen; at the present time they are concerned with themselves and their problems of development and relationship, but it seems more than likely that the next decade or so will see them more actively conscious of the room they live in, criticising it, rearranging it, enjoying it.

Non-fiction in New Zealand has not had nearly such a difficult time. Most of the early letters and diaries, written for private use only, had no trouble in giving faithful and immediate accounts of life in New Zealand, but even work written for publication achieved the freshness, the contact with reality, which fiction seemed unable to produce for so long. Frederick Manning's account of *Old New Zealand, by a Pakeha Maori* is still interesting and entertaining; it is a description of the period he spent living as a 'pakeha' Maori among Maoris, accepted by them as one of themselves. There has always been great interest in anthropological material of any sort dealing with the Maori race, and today's writers depend for their reconstructions upon accounts of the Maori written by missionaries, surveyors and other interested observers. Many of these old books have been considered worth reprinting and are available today, along with the works of Sir Peter Buck who has never gone out of print for any length of time.

New Zealand has been very fortunate in its historians. In the last twenty years much history has been written and that by extremely competent scholars. J. C. Beaglehole has made a distinguished contribution to the early history of the South Pacific, and much important work has been done on New Zealand history itself. Two good histories are now available as paperbacks, and the official War History contains some significant volumes, among them F. L. W. Wood's *The New Zealand People at War*, a valuable comment on the emergence of New Zealand as a country with responsibilities in the outside world. Much history, however, still remains to be written.

Perhaps it is a reflection of innate pragmatism that the New Zealander is least reluctant to buy books for which he can see some obvious use. Books on sport of all kinds have a ready market, especially those on the inside story of a rugby or cricket tour by a retiring participant or manager. Many books have been written on the mountains; tramping and out-of-doors material is very popular and easy to obtain. Some fine writers have made this their special field, enriching alike both active and passive high country trampers. New Zealanders are an outdoor people and books at all levels on natural history are eagerly sought. Some definitive botanical and geological accounts of New Zealand have been written and old books are being reprinted to fill the gaps. The Government Printer publishes much scientific material with a wide popular audience, as well as detailed local maps so necessary to the safety of trampers and mountaineers.

Newspapers in New Zealand are of a high standard but conservative in style and format. The coverage of world news is good although too dependent on overseas agencies. If there is little cultural content in local papers, there is also little gossip; not surprisingly, the papers are thin. Most of the larger provincial towns have their own privately owned newspapers. These papers provide local as well as national news and are little different from daily papers in the main cities. The political tone of practically all New Zealand newspapers is conservative.

All cultural activity has had an uphill road in New Zealand, but an indigenous play-writing tradition has been slowest of all to emerge. Early writing was of the sentimental, melodramatic variety and not until later in the twentieth century were some New Zealand playwrights successful overseas, although not often with plays based on New Zealand material. Douglas Stewart was the most important of these; some of his plays do use his experience as a New Zealander and many are still performed. Many recent writers have written one or two good plays but performances of them are usually few and far between, and are rarely ever seen at all outside the country. If New Zealanders are slow to write good plays about their country, they are not slow to act other plays. The emphasis has mainly been upon amateur performances; the population is not large enough consistently to support a professional theatre. The New Zealand Players group ran into financial difficulties after only eight years of existence and was finally wound up in 1960. More humble efforts at professional theatre have been tried from time to time in the main cities, but have often led a short, if merry, life. These companies have, however, greatly encouraged the production of local plays and have given considerable stimulus to writers in other fields to attempt the dramatic form. They have also strengthened the enthusiasm of the lively amateur theatrical movement which flourishes in New Zealand. Even some of the smallest towns boast an amateur Repertory Theatre, and their productions are often of a high standard. These groups present a wide range of drama, from the classical and conventional to the up-to-the-minute modern. Plays by New Zealanders are also given production; plays by Bruce Mason, Baxter and Sargeson have all been produced for small-town audiences. The British Drama League's one-act play festival competitions have stimulated great interest in one-act plays and local writers have produced some skilful works in this form.

The University Drama Clubs are enthusiastic and venturesome in their productions and the Community Arts Service of the Auckland Regional Council for Adult Education has toured the North Island with many productions. Professional companies from overseas visit New Zealand at fairly frequent intervals, which not only encourages local talent but also keeps audiences in touch with new techniques, new plays and new actors.

The Broadcasting Corporation has acted as godparent-cum-patron to New Zealand drama, producing numerous home-grown plays which would otherwise have been stillborn. Many new playwrights have appeared with this encouragement, although generally speaking the plays have been more competent than inspired. However,

The Tree, by Stella Jones, is a work of perception and beauty and Dora Somerville is writing radio plays of great excitement and insight.

As with drama, New Zealand ballet is largely a do-it-yourself enterprise which has achieved some surprising successes. Ballet has been taught in New Zealand for many years, but until quite recently talented dancers had to go overseas to get any experience of performing in live ballet. Some of these dancers were very good indeed; Rowena Jackson, Alexander Grant and Bryan Ashbridge, all of the Royal Ballet, are internationally renowned. A national ballet, however, was not established until 1954 under Poul Gnatt, but although its members were full of enthusiasm and devotion, the company was forced to struggle on a shoe-string existence for some years. Government and other theatrical bodies helped considerably where they could, but the Company began to make real progress only when substantial Government assistance was forthcoming from the Arts Advisory Council instituted in 1960. Overseas touring artists such as Beryl Grey and Margot Fonteyn have stimulated public interest in ballet, benefiting the Ballet Company enormously. The director, Poul Gnatt, has been able to build up an experienced body of dancers using as a nucleus New Zealanders returned from dancing abroad, and the works performed throughout the country have had a high professional polish. Other small ballet companies, such as the Wellington City Ballet, the United Ballet Company and the Ballet Workshop in Auckland, have all helped to sustain and develop public interest in the art.

Cultural activities have tended to be largely peripheral in New Zealand, and where they have flourished, it has been because of a small body of dedicated, often very talented amateurs, who have enthusiastically promoted a discipline in the face of discouraging lack of interest. The problem with musical, dramatic and artistic concerns is that normally it is the same small proportion of a small population which is interested and limited financial resources have to be stretched to cover all activities. Frequently artistic ventures, quite viable in a country with a bigger population, collapse because the resources of the interested community have been stretched too far. This occurred for many years in the field of music, where the amateur musician provided the only live music between visits of overseas artists. Not until 1946 was a National Orchestra finally set on its feet under the watchful eye of the Broadcasting Corporation. The

Orchestra has performed an unenviable task with energy and devotion; it tours the country regularly, bringing music to small provincial towns omitted from the itinerary of overseas artists, and constantly entertains, educates and stimulates a public very willing to be instructed. At the same time, its members have striven to improve the quality of their sound and increase the range of their repertoire. The Orchestra acts as a maid of all work to any amateur or semi-amateur body (such as choral and operatic societies) requiring orchestral accompaniment. The New Zealand Broadcasting Corporation Symphony Orchestra has meant a great deal in New Zealand's musical life, and has spurred on the growth of the National Youth Orchestra – a body of young players meeting once or twice a year for intensive orchestral instruction culminating in a series of public concerts. The National Orchestra also performs works by New Zealanders such as Douglas Lilburn, David Farquhar and Jenny MacLeod, a composer of international repute.

Chamber Music Societies are commonly found in sizeable towns in New Zealand. They promote visits from overseas chamber music artists and also provide an audience for performances by local players, many of whom have become technically competent. Choral groups also flourish, some of them founded very early in New Zealand's history. Between them they present a wide range of choral music; some of these choirs have remained in a nineteenth-century rut, but others have developed into very fine choirs in the modern tradition.

In 1954 the nucleus of a professional opera company was formed and it has since grown to a full-sized company which is slowly increasing its repertoire. Visiting experts have produced and directed some of the operas performed, helping the cast develop a sense of dramatic presence as well as musical technique. The Opera Company has been very fortunate in the singing teachers who have given a sound technical foundation to many singers of talent and promise. Most cities and provincial towns, but especially the latter, possess a Musical and Dramatic Society, a purely amateur affair which presents at least one full-scale musical comedy a year. The societies provide admirable chorus discipline which is valued by the Opera Company when it goes on tour; it relies heavily on building up its chorus strength from local talent wherever it visits, both to keep down expenses and to develop a widely distributed group of experienced singers. Also, the Musical and Dramatic Societies are an important link between the light musical tradition and more serious works; they help to emphasise the interdependence of music and drama in a light-hearted fashion ranging from Richard Strauss and Gilbert and Sullivan to modern American musicals. Unfortunately the success of these performances for a long time prevented popular appreciation and understanding of so-called 'grand' opera.

Although the subscription concerts of the National Orchestra and first nights of the Opera are normally well attended, New Zealanders in general seem to prefer their music light, and where possible they like to make it themselves. Up and down the country are to be found large numbers of high-quality brass bands and highland pipe bands. The activities of the Salvation Army have been responsible for getting boys and men interested in brass instruments; the Army bands have always been ready to teach promising beginners and to help them acquire instruments. Because the Salvation Army, especially during the first half of this century, had a uniformed brass band on the cold street corners of many cities and towns, bandsmanship spread into every part of New Zealand. This is a social and recreational activity as well as a cultural one – it is followed with much interest by many non-players, full of concern and parochial pride in the local lads and their band. Twice New Zealand has sent abroad a representative band, on both occasions winning high honours in international band circles. Highland pipe bands fulfil much the same function as brass bands, although there is also the glamour of the Scottish national dress which is worn by groups to enhance their popular appeal. There are also several women's pipe bands in New Zealand. Most of the larger towns sport at least one brass band and a pipe band as well, which become the focus of community sorrow or gaiety in times of national grief and rejoicing. Bands are very much part and parcel of the common life of the country.

Another do-it-yourself activity which has caught the imagination of ordinary people is pottery – perhaps this craft appeals to New Zealanders because of its functional nature. In any case, more and more people, mainly women, are learning the elements of pottery at night classes and polytechnics. Pottery seems to provide an elemental satisfaction of which people in an urban society frequently come to feel an urgent need. There are several professional potters in New Zealand and many others who work in a semi-professional capacity. The standard of work has risen greatly since New Zealand pottery was first exhibited, and while there is a long

way to go before the delicacy of a Lucy Ree is reached, or the
subtlety of glaze used by the Japanese masters, yet New Zealand
pottery can now stand as an art form in its own right. Some of the
best craftsmen are reaching out towards a greater sophistication of
shape, pattern and glaze; the market for this work is great and seems
to expand with every exhibition. This is one of the few arts which
has not required heavy Government subsidies for its support.

It has been suggested that pottery is but a country cousin to the
finer arts and that the glories of sculpture, painting and drawing
overshadow it completely. In New Zealand, at any rate, this is very
questionable. In painting and portraiture New Zealand probably
finds itself more insular, out of date and parochial than in any other
form of cultural activity. It is hard to see just why this should be,
unless the techniques of stimulating the mind travel more easily
than those which satisfy and delight the eye. As in literature, there
has been that debilitating backward glance towards the tradition of
British and European art which has fettered New Zealand artistic
endeavour to a sentimental and vague Victorianism, long discarded
in England itself. The early tendency towards sentiment and emo-
tion was given a special emphasis in New Zealand by the magni-
ficence of the natural scenery which provided, and still provides, the
main subject for artistic expression. Some of the early surveyors
made sketches which have much historical interest today but which
can hardly be considered great art; they do, however, represent the
first and last objective look at New Zealand for very many years.
Charles Heaphy is probably the best known of the early surveyors-
cum-artists – his sketches of early Wellington are merely interesting,
but his painting of milling in a kauri forest is very fine indeed.
Many other surveyors also made sketches and watercolours, but
their interests were more concerned with the topography of the
country than with an artistic expression of it. However, they may
well have laid the foundations for a purely New Zealand approach
to art if they had remained in the country. Unfortunately they
nearly all moved away, and New Zealand was left to the drawing-
room school of art favoured by most of the settlers with any degree
of refinement.

The greatest problem besetting those who did try to cope with
what they saw before their eyes (as opposed to what they thought
they should see) was that of light. In England, the light was softer
and the hills themselves more rounded, and consequently cast

gentler shadows. In New Zealand the sunlight is exceedingly bright and the outlines of the high hills and steep gorges very strong and harsh; the colour of the bush was also unaccustomed and very elusive. It took a long time for artists to adjust to these different conditions, just as it had taken the novelists a long time to learn to use New Zealand material unselfconsciously. Because New Zealand is a country full of remarkable scenery, where few people live away from the shadow of great hills or far from breathtaking views of the sea, the artists of the nineteenth and much of the twentieth centuries concentrated almost exclusively upon producing photographic representations of the country's spectacular scenic features. This sort of art was very popular in the community, especially the drawings and watercolours of John Gully, an early artist of considerable pretension but less ability. He made a deep impression on the course of New Zealand art, however, and many local artists continued happily in his footsteps, churning out studio paintings of outdoor scenes according to a well-defined formula.

As the country developed and prospered, schools of art were founded, first in Dunedin and later in the other main centres. Art societies soon followed in many places, the Wellington Art Society equipping itself with the grandiloquent but utterly misleading title of 'The New Zealand Academy of Fine Arts' – a name which it has kept until this day. These societies taught and practised the principles of English middle-class art, to the great detriment of artistic progress. Much needed stimulation was given by the arrival of two teachers, the Scotsman Nairn, and the Dutch artist van der Velden. Neither of these men was more than a competent artist, but they were devoted and careful teachers; New Zealand art took on a new shape and promise under their influence and many artists left New Zealand to continue their study in European art circles.

Up to the First World War, New Zealand had little that could be considered an indigenous artistic achievement. Two artists became widely known for their portraits; both Lindauer and Goldie made many fine studies of Maori heads. Goldie was probably the first New Zealand artist to become known overseas, but this was due more to his unusual models than to an extraordinary artistic ability. However, as in literature, the Second World War was a turning point in the development of New Zealand art. The post-war period was a time of experimentation and innovation – some of the experiments were wild and woolly rather than artistically constructive, but apart from a small glimmer of impressionism in the late nineteenth century, this was the first sign of artistic experiment New Zealand had ever seen. It was very welcome. The artists of the time were struggling with much the same problems as the poets of the thirties. It continues to be very difficult to paint landscapes without recourse to the European tradition; that is, to paint landscapes in a form more obviously dictated by the New Zealand than the English mind. After the Second War it became apparent that the writers had completely solved their problem; present-day painting suggests that New Zealand artists are still struggling, that they are full of vigour and promise, but that they have not yet quite arrived.

There is no lack of interest in art – amateur art societies abound – and it is relatively easy for an artist to arrange an exhibition of his work. Art in New Zealand is in a living state, largely because better teaching is available in art schools than was previously the case, and also because New Zealand's sense of isolation from the rest of the world is beginning to break down. Many artists paint in an abstract idiom, feeling their way to an effective emotional representation of society. Unfortunately, it is necessary to be a very fine artist to communicate in an abstract form, just as it requires an assured command of words to write in the stream-of-consciousness technique.

Landscapes appear to be the main artistic expression in New Zealand, usually with a traditional and slightly out-of-date quality which is disturbing when modern Canadian or American landscapes are recalled. However, New Zealanders are still a country people and conservative country people at that. It will be a long time before that sympathy and appreciation develop towards modern New Zealand art which is already apparent towards modern New Zealand poetry. Colin McCahon and Peter McIntyre are the most prominent New Zealand artists today – McCahon is an expressionist/abstract painter, and Peter McIntyre is a mass producer of competent landscapes for public consumption (which is not to say that he has not done some very fine work indeed). Frances Hodgkins is probably the most able painter New Zealand has yet produced, and the one most likely to be familiar to people overseas. Like Katherine Mansfield, whose contemporary she was, she left New Zealand permanently having tasted the vigour and stimulation of the European artistic community. Her work stands firmly in the European tradition and it is as a European impressionist that she must now be judged. It is perhaps unrealistic of New Zealand to claim her as an artist; there are, however, times when local pride may be allowed to overwhelm other considerations.

Only a small amount of sculpture has been done in New Zealand, and that only recently. Few works of an imaginative and stimulating nature have ever been commissioned; public bodies have up until the present time been conservatively content with dull memorials to public figures. However, a small group of modern sculptors is busy exploring the possibilities of the medium in terms of modern New Zealand, an encouraging development which says a great deal for the initiative and determination of these artists.

All cultural activities in New Zealand have begun on the initiative of individuals, and until very recently, have remained on an amateur or semi-amateur basis. New Zealand became a welfare state early in its history because only Government possessed the resources to provide the help required by some sections of the population. In much the same way, although very reluctantly, Government took over the duties of patron towards all cultural endeavour. Quite early it supported the establishment of libraries and subsidised their maintenance, but this could be regarded as a function of education and therefore obviously useful. It was also ready to legislate that local governments should support museums, to help preserve priceless Maori artifacts, but it was very slow to come to the rescue of art galleries in the same way, even though there was no other alternative. Not until after the Second World War did the Government succumb to consistent pressure for large-scale support for the arts in New Zealand; it had helped before in small ways, by subsidising the literary quarterly *Landfall* and providing music and drama bursaries for exceptionally talented people to train overseas. However, after a long period of hole-in-the-corner trial and error, the Government established the Queen Elizabeth II Arts Council to commemorate the visit to New Zealand of the Queen and the Duke of Edinburgh in 1964. Already grants from this body have made a big difference to activities such as the National Ballet and the Opera Company; it also provides an increased number of bursaries for overseas study and has made its presence felt in other useful ways. The achievement of all artists who struggled alone against the problems of public apathy, isolation and a lack of stimulation has been of inestimable value in the developing culture of New Zealand. In 1967, after just over a hundred and twenty years of European settlement, New Zealanders can be said to be embarking upon the creation of a culture which is not only unique but which expresses clearly the bond between the artist and his society.

Perhaps the most telling expression of New Zealand culture, state of mind and outlook, can be seen in the country's architecture. When they first arrived, the settlers and their families lived in small cottages made of cob (a clay and straw mixture) or of 'wattle and daub', puddled clay slapped on to a sapling framework. These cottages were roofed with thatch or wooden shingles or even with tussock, and the floors were usually made of hard-packed mud. The old cob cottages were very strong and weatherproof and there are still a few of these buildings standing firm and watertight in odd corners of the country. These cottages were soon superseded by the wooden houses which the settlers built for themselves on their new farmlands – by the 1850's some quite fine wooden houses had been built. The key to the pleasant proportion of these houses lies in the constant discipline of form to the demands of function. Timber was the only plentiful material, and the early builders were forced, willy-nilly, into a form which had great strength and beauty of proportion. The permanent cottages derived strongly from the 'but and ben' cottage to be found all over England and Scotland. Built in heart totara, kauri or rimu timber this proved a flexible unit for a growing family and could take additions without loss of proportion.

Another form of house, larger and usually single-storied, was the early colonial 'box', a wooden frame house often exactly square, with a passage down the middle and four symmetrical rooms on each side. At the back of the house it was common to add a lean-to kitchen and bathroom. By this time people had adjusted to the strong, bright light of New Zealand, and verandahs supported by slim timber uprights frequently surrounded the 'box' on three sides. The front door opened off the verandah directly on to the hall, and on each side of the door were large double-hung windows. Again, this was a very flexible structure, as portions of the side verandahs could be easily enclosed to make more rooms as the family increased.

Both these types of house sat in pleasant harmony in their New Zealand surroundings, either on open tussock lands or in heavy bush. For many years, probably until well after New Zealand celebrated its centenary, they formed the most satisfying expression of indigenous architecture. Their success lay mainly in their simplicity and lack of pretence, although they were not without a certain elegance of their own. Many houses of this sort, especially the 'box' type, are still used as family homes today.

As the country developed and the population grew in numbers and prosperity, more complicated variations of these early homes were built. All additional embroidery on the basic pattern was heavily derivative from English domestic architecture; the 'modern' style in New Zealand, at least until the First World War, lagged well behind the latest trends in England. House decoration and ornamentation became an accepted status-symbol and pseudo-Gothic gargoyles appeared incongruously in wood dressed up as stone, accompanied in time by much indifferent wrought-iron work.

From about 1913, 'bungalow' houses of different varieties were fashionable and many were built throughout the country. These houses are not beautiful nor even convenient to live in but their smaller size was ideal for a country where servants vanished earlier than anywhere else in the world. Until recently only in a few private homes have New Zealanders attempted to design for a specifically New Zealand way of life, bringing as much open air living into the home as the climate permits and catering for all aspects of family activity. Comparatively few private homes are architect designed, but builders and home planners are beginning to use techniques of design developed in other countries – especially America. More and more homes are being built incorporating these ideas, and although the outside view of a modern house is box-like to a distressing degree, the interior is frequently extraordinarily comfortable. Like the Englishman, the New Zealander regards his home as his castle, but although his home, standing in its neat section, is usually well maintained and very respectable, little is done to make it a private retreat from the outside world. Some cities, such as Wellington and Dunedin, have an inherent advantage in that most homes are built on sloping sections which can be used to provide privacy; but even here little use has been made of natural advantages. New Zealand has such a good climate for the growth of exotic trees that everyone can possess the benefit of privacy with a little effort – and laziness is not one of the New Zealander's sins. Apparently, therefore, privacy is a peripheral desirability, or else New Zealanders are not sufficiently imaginative to plan for it.

Modern State houses, built by the Government for tenant occupation, are not usually inspiring versions of domestic architecture although great efforts have been made to prevent an overriding uniformity in any one district; these have been only partially successful. However, these houses have a high standard of modern convenience, if they lack external beauty, and can be constructed relatively quickly. The State also supplies to its tenants materials for hedges and shrub screens, in order to offset as much as possible the disadvantages of collective housing and to help provide privacy in an area of comparatively high population density.

Public architecture in New Zealand has followed much the same course as domestic building. Of necessity the first public buildings were very simple, small in size and limited in scope by the lack of building materials other than timber. Nevertheless, they incorporated in their design a considerable beauty of proportion which enhanced the public dignity of their function. As the country progressed these buildings naturally became too small for comfort, and were replaced by more grandiloquent statements of public office. These buildings, many of which remain today, are still small by overseas standards, but by and large, have lost that spare simplicity which marked their predecessors. Ornamentation, as in home building, was used to indicate status and importance; some public buildings were so overcome with pseudo-Gothic detail that they became a positive hazard in times of earthquakes. The present General Assembly Library is an awe-inspiring example of Gothic run wild, and deserves to be preserved if only as a warning to future generations. However, while such monstrosities were being perpetrated, the old wooden tradition was not quite lost. The spare symmetry of the Government Departmental Building, said to be the largest wooden building in the Southern Hemisphere, is still an ornament to its site and a delight to look upon. Its greatest drawback lies in its high maintenance costs.

The danger of over-ornamented buildings in earthquakes was a lesson to be heeded, especially after the Napier earthquake in 1931. Public taste has also changed, and most buildings erected since the war have exploited the materials of steel, concrete and glass in the curtain wall block, which is not without its disadvantages in the bright light of New Zealand. It is also an undeniably anonymous form of architecture, although some of the best examples are pleasant to see. Perhaps the main advantage of the curtain wall construction is that it requires great ability to make it positively ugly. There are recent signs, however, that New Zealand architects are branching out into more entertaining, yet restrained and tasteful, forms of large buildings.

New Zealand ecclesiastical architecture has followed much the same course as domestic and public building. The early missionaries were their own architects, and Selwyn and Thatcher evolved a very simple satisfying church, reminiscent of the simplest stone Gothic in England, but in New Zealand of course constructed in timber, giving a mellow texture of great beauty. These churches were designed with high pitched roofs and steeples; some even had tiny transepts and supporting buttresses in the best Gothic tradition. Churches built for Maori worship were largely improvisations. The missionaries clung to the high pitched roof, and adapted cruciform with sanctuary and nave, though the transepts were often omitted, but upon this fabric was imposed all the tradition of Maori life. The old Maori churches which still exist are tributes to a harmonious union of cultures.

The middle years of the country saw the construction of much bigger churches, though not necessarily better ones from an architectural point of view. Heavily Gothic and deliberately European, these were built in wood, stone or brick – the brick ones probably the least successful and now fortunately covered over with the all-concealing ivy. Modern liturgical developments have led to fundamental changes in church architecture, and some exciting churches have been built in the last ten years, using new opportunities offered by modern materials previously considered unsuitable for ecclesiastical use.

Many of the older provincial centres and small towns still bear the faded marks of the frontiers they once were. Shops and offices remain with false fronts, trying to make themselves more imposing than they really are, and the overhanging street verandahs, roofed with corrugated iron and supported with timber posts, provide reminders of an age that has not yet really gone, although it is undoubtedly on the way out. In short, the picture presented by New Zealand architecture today gives an accurate history of the life of the country and in doing so gives some measure of the New Zealander's innate conservatism and lack of imagination. However, when he is forced to branch out and improvise, his building is remarkable for its flexibility and lack of pretence. His architecture is very like his political thinking and in itself emphasises the strengths and weaknesses of the society from which it springs.

Chapter 9

Bi-Racial Society

T HE EARLY SETTLERS in New Zealand were an interesting group, covering a surprisingly wide social range. There were the gentility, Wakefield's aristocracy, who were to set the tone and standard of the Colony and were to remain a privileged class. Some of these immigrants were indeed members of the English aristocracy, and although many of them quickly returned home when they saw that the colonial utopia had yet to be created, some did remain. There were also a fair number of middle-class immigrants who in many cases came to New Zealand because of a financial failure at home. All these settlers brought with them the incalculable benefits of a well-founded education and many came with money in their pockets as well. Generally speaking the ratio of educated to uneducated people was higher in New Zealand than in England itself. They worked hard and gave generously of their energies and talents to the small communities in which they lived. Their contribution to early New Zealand was very great, but their lives were not as rigorous as those of many immigrants. Jessie Campbell, the wife of a well-to-do Wanganui settler, wrote in 1843: 'The last time I wrote I was very much harassed, being without a servant for two months. I did the whole work of the home, except the washing. I have one now . . .' In 1845 she wrote some illuminating comments: 'We had the honour of a call from the Bishop. He is so handsome and fascinating that while he was present I forgot my prejudice against him on account of his Puseyite doctrine. . . . He is very zealous certainly in his exertions among the Maoris but like most of our authorities he has too exalted an opinion of them, and seems to forget that tho' intelligent they are but savages. . . .'

The other settlers mostly came from the English lower middle class, small men who could see no hope for themselves or their families in the England of their day. A large number of immigrants came from Scotland, not all to live in the Presbyterian settlement of Otago. They came because the hopeless position of tenant farmers downtrodden by agents of absentee landlords could not be made worse by such a radical departure, and might perhaps be improved. These people came, in common with those who considered themselves their betters, because New Zealand seemed a country of opportunity and hope – the hope that they and their families might live better lives, and by better they meant socially improved lives. To this end they laboured desperately hard. The reminiscences of Sarah Higgins of Nelson help to explain how painful the struggle was for Wakefield's 'peasants'. Sarah came to New Zealand at the age of twelve with her father and her brothers. They settled in Nelson as members of the New Zealand Company's colony there, and an inhospitable time of it they had. After the Wairau massacre, the wealthier settlers fled. Sarah recalled: 'Well, then our troubles began. There was no food, no money. There were no shops to get anything. We had to get fern roots and berries, sow thistles and docks and boil them. . . . They were very hard times. The men got so [weak] they could not work except for a few hours at a time. . . .'

Life improved for Sarah Higgins, but it never rose to the primitive elegance of that of Jessie Campbell. As in England, so in New Zealand there was always a social gap, but it is significant that in spite of the gulf that existed then, and indeed still exists today, the labouring men and the small farmers without independent means doffed the cap to no one, not even their employers. Visitors from England found this regrettable and odd, accompanied as it frequently was by a conscious lack of subservience bordering upon the uncivil. Every man felt, and still feels, as good as every other man, even although outward appearances might well be to the contrary. This, along with a social fluidity which allowed a man to better himself if he wished, was the cornerstone of New Zealand's developing society. What has finally emerged is as classless a society as it is possible to find anywhere – classless, because from the beginning everyone was forced to belong, to a greater or lesser degree, to the same class. Sarah Higgins had much in common with Jessie Campbell and although the gulf which yawned between them was wide, in New Zealand, at least, it could be bridged.

The outward classlessness of society may explain the marked conformity of New Zealand life. There is little room for the odd or eccentric either in character or in taste; indeed, only since the end of the war have professional artists and writers been granted a tolerant hearing. The mainspring of conformity is perhaps the New

Zealander's original desire to have social equality at all costs, even when this might be more apparent than real. All are running the race, and all must have prizes, preferably the same prizes. The result is a way of life easy enough to condemn from the outside. New Zealanders live in rows of similar houses, predictably furnished in the fashions of their several generations, with little or no deviation from shop display windows. In the country farmhouses often perpetuate the modern city box, incongruously planted in the middle of a bare paddock like some strange pastel-coloured growth. The inhabitants of the houses live apparently similar lives, especially in the cities; sport on Saturday for the men, followed by a visit to the pub – a male preserve – and on Sunday gardening, cleaning the car and the family outing in the afternoon. A quiet, domestic people, New Zealanders, seeking a certain security in the safety of conformity.

But beneath the quiet surface, New Zealanders lead an extra-ordinarily varied existence. In common with individuals in any urban society, many men work at jobs in which they are barely interested let alone fulfilled, but in New Zealand it is surprising how many such people have remarkable hobbies. Scratch a clerk, and it is quite possible to find an expert on practically anything. There are self-taught astronomers watching the heavens through amateur telescopes, there are horticulturists with a knowledge of hybridising as great as that of any expert; many men design and build ocean-going yachts in their back gardens. This man is a fount of wisdom on all the train systems in the world, that man designs, builds and drives racing cars. Most of these spare-time activities are of a practical nature, but there are also people tucked away in un-likely corners of the country who are authorities on everything from Japanese scroll painting to early musical instruments. These more esoteric hobbies are usually kept out of sight until the practitioner is sure of his audience, but the very presence of these people in the community adds a current of unexpected excitement to the sluggish flow of the mainstream.

The mainstream is indeed sluggish, and for several complicated reasons. The most important one has its roots in the history of European occupation and the struggle of the early farmers to subdue their land and make it yield a livelihood. The land itself was obdurate, very different from the tamed and peaceful farmlands of England. Life for the farmer and his family was lonely and hard, and most were exhausted with the effort of wresting from the land the good things they had come so far to obtain. In the towns, also, New Zealand developed a society dominated by 'things' just as it remains today. Until at least 1900 there were many good reasons why New Zealand should develop a materialistic culture. After all, the more goods and chattels a man possessed, the more successful he could be seen to be. This has always been the case in any country, but in New Zealand it meant not just that a certain standard of wealth had been achieved, but that a man and his family had been successful in the struggle for existence, for very life itself. This was especially so before the gold rushes, which bore eloquent testimony to the importance of tangible wealth, a lesson bitterly recalled during the terrible years of the Long Depression in the eighteen-eighties and nineties. Society grew and evolved as the country developed, but it remained firmly orientated towards the possession of objects. The 'good' life, which the community considered the right of everyone, was symbolised first by the basic possessions of human existence — shelter, food, clothes and a certain security in keeping these things. As the years passed, the basic commodities of life expanded and became shorthand status-symbols. With the whole force of society and its economy concentrating on this aspect of life, it was not long before possessions themselves became the pivot of existence. They were no longer the symbols of a 'good' or satisfying life; they were the good life itself. Perhaps this is the reason why New Zealanders strive so hard to equip themselves with all the useful — especially the useful — and entertaining products of man's ingenuity. The country stands among the first half-dozen in the world on a *per capita* count of telephones, washing machines, automobiles, refrigerators, juice extractors, vacuum cleaners, power drills, television sets and so on. In itself, this is a good thing; it is a bleak prospect indeed that fills life with the back-breaking drudgery of Sarah Higgins. The question for New Zealanders now, as for other affluent, materialistic cultures, is — Where do we go from here? The answer may well lie in the impulse, now that time is a servant and not the ruthless master that early New Zealanders knew, to go back and pick up those gentler, less pragmatic arts of civilisation which were necessarily put to one side as men won for themselves the right to live in New Zealand at all, and which have been largely neglected ever since.

The mainstream of New Zealand society is sluggish for another reason, which also explains the country's reluctance to take up the cultivation which it so decisively laid aside in the last century. Generally speaking, the settlers arrived from England imbued with the evangelical theology of humanitarianism upheld by a Puritan admiration of hard work and such sobriety as fortified the colonists of New England. A certain dourness runs through the New Zealand character, perhaps a legacy from so many Scottish forebears. In any case, from the beginning of established settlement, especially in Otago and the New Zealand Company settlements, a peculiar dreariness shaped the country's habits and practices. Everyone was too hard-working to play, and if they were not too busy, they should have been. Today, New Zealand could scarcely be called a religious country, but it has suited the people to maintain some of the old institutions, though sectional protests against them may well be gaining ground. Sunday is still a day of rest. Some people go to church, but more are occupied around their homes, competently doing themselves those jobs for which they cannot afford to pay tradesmen. All quality restaurants and public houses are shut, except for coffee bars and the public dining-rooms of hotels. Shops are shut, apart from suburban dairies, and so are all places of amusement — except, maybe, the zoo. Sideshows, theatres, concert halls, billiard and snooker saloons, all fall into a proper Sabbatarian quiet. There are no competitive public sports. The population is at rest, not, in 1967, because of its religious convictions, but because it enjoys the day of peace and the opportunity to do things as individuals. This is a happy state for New Zealanders, but a lamentable discovery for strangers in the country. Once he has read the two Sunday news-papers — a recent innovation — he has reached the end of New Zealand's Sunday resources.

Good Friday is a day almost without activity at all. People do what they wish, but most shops open on a Sunday are usually shut and there is no postal delivery and no newspaper. Even to an irreligious community, this still seems right and proper and there is no pressure to brighten up the day. This is not the case with ANZAC Day, however. ANZAC Day is a public holiday to commemorate the landing of the Australia and New Zealand Army Corps on the beaches of Gallipoli — a day of disaster for so many New Zealand families. It has been kept with all the wailing pomp and splendour of a grieving nation ever since, but now most of the men who fought in the First World War are dead and many soldiers of the Second World War would prefer to forget and enjoy what life is offering now. The year 1915 was a long time ago; it now seems time merely to commemorate ANZAC Day in passing.

Another manifestation of the Puritan outlook is New Zealand's archaic licensing laws. Drink was a menace in New Zealand from the earliest days and throughout the country small groups of temperance reformers and prohibitionists attempted to dissuade a largely deaf populace from the evils of liquor. Strongly supported by the Protestant churches, these groups made little impact until the 1860's when most Provinces passed licensing regulations in an endeavour to counteract the upsurge of drunkenness. The cause of prohibition was actively supported by the New Zealand Alliance for the Suppression and Prohibition of the Liquor Traffic, founded in 1886. The views of the Alliance were self-evident, although today the same body does not seek to prohibit but merely to lessen the amount of liquor consumed. When it was founded, the Alliance was supported by many worthy men and a great number of women – the women were astute enough to use the movement as a springboard towards female suffrage, and were so successful that New Zealand women received the vote nearly a quarter of a century before those in other parts of the world. The Liberal Government under Seddon was forced into liquor legislation by outside pressure and by Sir Robert Stout's breakaway group inside the party. In 1893 the Alcoholic Liquor Sales Control Act was passed, giving New Zealand the system which, with alarmingly few modifications, is operated to this day. Historically, the sale of liquor had generally been connected with the provision of accommodation – a natural situation in a sparsely populated country with long distances between settlements. A Licensing Commission was set up to scrutinize the licences of hotel-keepers and to control the issue of new ones. Today a Commission does much the same work, although licences have recently been extended to high-class restaurants. The electorate was given the opportunity to regulate the local liquor situation at the triennial political elections, a custom which still persists. Public interest in the enforcement of prohibition faded markedly after the First World War, although the New Zealand Alliance and the Women's Christian Temperance Union still believe that most of mankind should be propelled into a state of sobriety by its elders and betters. Fortunately, New Zealand escaped the disaster of complete prohibition, but large parts of the country at one time or another went 'dry' under the influence of campaigning prohibitionists. Whenever this happened, the sly grog trade flourished, and much 'home-brew' or do-it-yourself beer was made. In some areas, particularly on the west coast and in Otago, there were some illegal but very active stills, producing a highly intoxicating beverage known throughout the country as 'hokonui'. However, at the present time very few parts of the country are 'dry', and these are mostly the suburban areas of the larger towns.

In recent times, the activities of the Alliance have served merely to strengthen hotel and brewery interests by consistently supporting six o'clock closing. This particular feature of New Zealand life must be experienced to be believed, as large numbers of men crowd themselves into the confined space of public bars with a phrenetic determination to drink as much as possible before the pub shuts. Everything about the process is unpleasant, the noise, the heat, the standing room only – the one redeeming feature is probably the beer itself. New Zealanders drink twenty-two gallons of beer per head – man, woman and child – each year, something like seventy million gallons in all. Appreciable quantities of spirits and wine are also consumed, although not usually by the man-in-the-street, who depends upon the half gallon flagon of draught beer for his after hours refreshment. It is only fair to add that drunkenness as such is probably decreasing, whereas alcoholism, in common with most other Western countries, is increasing alarmingly.

Liquor in New Zealand is big business and almost all hotels are controlled, if not owned, by one or other of the big breweries. Brewing itself is highly monopolistic, and brewery shares in New Zealand have taken on the qualities of 'gilt-edged' investments. Brewery domination of the retail side of the trade has not been entirely a bad thing because without such large financial resources very little licensed accommodation of any sort would be available except in the main centres. On the other hand, hotel services based upon the profits of the liquor trade have considerably obscured the possibility of making the provision of accommodation in itself a profitable activity. Accommodation to cater for New Zealand's rising tourist trade has suffered accordingly.

The Alliance, however, does strongly support the establishment of Trust Hotels. Licensing Trusts are *ad hoc*, non profit-making bodies set up to retail liquor within a given locality at the express wish of the electors. Once established a Trust has a monopoly in its area and the profits are used to improve drinking facilities or given to local good causes.

Only in the country, and not always there, can the public bar be considered a place of community relaxation, and then it is a purely male affair. Women have been socially if not legally excluded from such places since the bad old days, although a sign of the changing times may be the reintroduction of a few barmaids. New Zealand's licensing laws provide an eloquent reminder that serious settlement began only 120 years ago; such pockets of social custom perpetuate in the modern world some of the attitudes and conditions of the frontier colony.

Another remnant of the frontier days is a parochial antagonism between town and country which dates from the 1860's at least. The gold rush and the ensuing boom brought to New Zealand a wave of unskilled workers with neither the wherewithal nor the inclination to buy land. As the main centres grew larger, their inhabitants naturally demanded a greater share in the government of the country and with the advent of the Liberal Administration towards the end of the last century they achieved this to a certain extent. Equally inevitably, the towns became identified with left-wing elements whereas the prosperous farming community remained essentially conservative in its outlook. In good times antagonism is latent, although urban dwellers envy the greater share of the national income that generally accrues to the farmers at such times. When the economy is depressed, however, the divorce between the two interests becomes more obvious and farmers are very conscious that their costs, mainly determined by the level of town wages, do not fall as much as their income. In times of economic stress, New Zealand can ill afford such a clash of sectional interests, leading as it does to strife only too quickly reflected in social legislation.

Yet for the most part New Zealand society is very stable and this is at least partly attributable to the fact that most people own their own homes. Home ownership has for many years been a major social goal and today there are very few houses available for letting on a long-term basis. The possession of a suburban villa with lawns, hedges and a garden to look after, not to mention the fabric of the house itself and the ubiquitous car, is undoubtedly conducive to social stability if not culture. Most people have to borrow heavily to acquire their first home but they have half a lifetime as a rule to pay it off. Appreciation of property values has been very marked in most localities in the last fifteen years and people on the 'up' commonly leapfrog from house to house using the profit from the sale of one as deposit on another, bigger, brighter and better. Since expenditure on repairs and maintenance is not deductible for income tax purposes, the incentive for the owner to effect them himself is great, however limited his practical skills, even if he could earn a substantially greater sum by otherwise employing his time. The repayment of home mortgages is much the most important form of saving for the great majority of people and this naturally gives rise to extreme reluctance to change jobs where this means shifting from an area where property values are depressed.

Two disturbing features of the contemporary scene are the rising illegitimacy rate, coupled with an increasing incidence of venereal disease. Both, it appears, stem largely from greater promiscuity among young people. The proportion of illegitimate births to the total births has jumped alarmingly in the last few years, but this is largely due to a drop in legitimate births as the use of oral contraceptives has become widespread. Nevertheless, the number of illegitimate births has continued to rise when it could have been expected to fall. This is probably partly the result of making oral contraceptives available only on a doctor's prescription, but it also indicates a more libertarian attitude towards sex.

It has also resurrected a problem which most New Zealanders thought buried for ever. Until the recent increase in illegitimate births, unwanted children were nearly all adopted; there are at the present time few orphanages and children's homes in the country. Now the number of children for adoption has far outdistanced the demand and provision for these children will soon become an urgent necessity. While the State is prepared to provide for the results of the community's promiscuity, it is very reluctant to take any effective steps to sanction adequate sexual education for schoolchildren, steps which might prevent some at least of these social tragedies. At the present time, sexual instruction is not given at school, nor, apparently, is it forthcoming from parents. It is easy to appreciate the State's reluctance to assume yet another responsibility for the individual, but pilot schemes integrating sexual education with general instruction on the art of living have been very successful. On a purely practical level, the cost of such education is much less than the cost of maintaining illegitimate children.

Although most weddings in New Zealand are still celebrated in church, the sense of indissolubility of marriage has long been lost.

New Zealand was originally ahead of most countries in legislating for divorce and recently an Act has been passed to allow the courts to grant a divorce even where the 'innocent' party opposes it. The generally easier requirements for divorce by consent have undoubtedly made divorce more common but at the same time have probably reduced the number of unhappy marriages. The connection between broken homes and juvenile delinquency is of course as strong in New Zealand as elsewhere. A further social problem is developing in the increasing number of wives who voluntarily leave their husbands. Usually these women seek a divorce, but although the husband must support the children the wives are entitled to no maintenance for themselves. Many such women are quite unqualified to perform any but the most menial work, and have no financial resources behind them. Regardless of the rights and wrongs of the case, separated women with families have to find new homes and continue the business of living; some assistance will probably have to be granted by the State.

More and more married women are offering themselves for employment, some for obviously economic reasons, as soon as their children go to primary school, and some for more complicated reasons, after their children have gone to secondary school. A generation of women is now becoming available for more than just passing employment because they married young and their children are off their hands, leaving between ten and twenty years of working life ahead of them. They also find that working is a pleasant release from the rather mindless domestic demands made by a growing family. The employment opportunities of women depend largely on their education and training before marriage; some women return to their previous occupations, but many would like to branch out into different fields. New Zealand has been slow to provide retraining opportunities for its growing female work force; where women have gone back and deliberately retrained themselves for some specific occupation, their greater maturity and experience have given them an enormous advantage over young people just out of school. These women have a great deal to contribute to the community, but the number who have managed to do this, compared with the number who would like to, is small. Many women of lower educational standards have found employment in factories and shops and as domestic labour. The remuneration is quite high, and because of the labour shortage which has existed since the war, employers are willing to make complicated part-time arrangements. Competent typists are at a premium, but women who have run a home and family are reluctant to return to office routine. Equal pay for men and women in the State services and the diffused effects of this elsewhere have encouraged women to return to some sort of employment, part-time or otherwise, but much more can be done to help re-educate women so that they can contribute more to the economic development of the country.

Formal education in New Zealand is very much a State preserve, as might be expected from the country's long history of Government intervention in social and economic affairs. Private schools exist but they function under the severe handicap of virtually no assistance from the State, either for buildings or staff, in a country where personal income tax is high and exemptions for school fees are purely nominal. It is not therefore surprising that the great majority of children attend State schools, unless their parents are wealthy or Roman Catholics. By and large the standards of instruction and the facilities at State schools are superior to those of private schools, mainly because of the financial difficulties faced by the latter. Towards the end of last century education was highly controversial and the 1877 Act provided for 'free, secular and compulsory' education in a State system of primary schools, although parents were allowed to send their children to private schools approved by the Education Department. The dust of this sectarian controversy is not entirely settled yet because of dissident opinions in two strongly opposed camps. The Roman Catholic Church, with some support from other religious groups, naturally desires State aid whereas non-Christians oppose even the limited voluntary undenominational Bible instruction now given in State schools, generally by outsiders who are allowed into the schools for half an hour a week.

Education is compulsory between the ages of seven and fifteen years but most children start their formal schooling at five and finish at about sixteen. Pre-school instruction is catered for by kindergartens and play centres; the former operated by the State, the latter by parent co-operatives. Primary schools cater for the first eight years of formal education, usually in the same school, although in larger centres the last two years are spent in intermediate schools. Promotion within the primary school system is normally automatic and at the age of thirteen or thereabouts, depending on date of birth, children proceed to secondary schools irrespective of their academic attainments. Primary schools are administered by regional Education Boards but in all important matters the Education Department controls the system.

All fully fledged secondary schools are, however, administered by Boards of Governors and in general the Education Department has far less control over the secondary school system. Whereas New Zealand primary schools have been happy hunting grounds for educational theorists, secondary schools have always been much more traditional and conservative. This is shown by the retention of formal academic and competitive examinations despite efforts to abolish them in the interests of 'better adjusted citizens'. Since New Zealand as a whole is strikingly non-competitive (except in sport) many people regard this residual element of competition as desirable whatever its theoretical weaknesses. In principle there are no grades of secondary schools but in practice some are much more strongly orientated towards academic studies than others. Nearly all State secondary schools, however, offer a wide variety of courses and almost all courses enable children to sit the national School Certificate examination at the end of the third or fourth year. In many cases those who are successful remain at school for a further year, or more, in order to qualify for entrance to university. Both single sex and mixed schools exist.

The university entrance qualification may be obtained either by accrediting one year after passing the School Certificate examination, or by examination in the case of those not accredited. Since the possession of the bare entrance qualification is often insufficient for success at the university, an increasing proportion of secondary school pupils stay a further year and many sit a competitive examination that entitles those doing well in it to financial assistance with their university studies. Everyone passing university entrance is entitled to free tuition except where subjects have to be repeated but the possession of a scholarship or bursary also carries with it grants towards living expenses.

There are now six universities but few offer a complete range of faculties. Arts and science are of course taught at all, law and commerce at most, engineering and agriculture at some, but so far there is only one medical school. The heavy hand of the Education Department is less in evidence at the universities but they are almost entirely dependent on Government for building and salaries. Thus explicit Government approval is required for all major buildings and the Government sets salary scales. With the post-war population explosion and the marked trend towards higher education, the Government has been forced to spend large sums on the universities in recent years but salaries, facilities for research and teaching, and staff to student ratios all compare unfavourably with universities in Australia and other countries.

Tertiary education outside universities is now receiving some attention after many years of neglect. Polytechnics have been established in the main centres but they enjoy far less autonomy than the universities. Teacher training in New Zealand is handled by teachers' colleges with a two-year course for non-graduates and a one-year course for graduates. A move towards three-year courses for non-graduates (primary school teachers) is now under way despite the well founded objection that it is more important to reduce size of classes. The calibre of teacher college staffs is not generally very high because until recently this position was ill-rewarded.

New Zealand society is enriched beyond measure by the presence of the rapidly growing Maori population. The Maoris have such a different cultural heritage from the pakeha that the problems of a peaceful bi-racial society are very complicated; whether the country will develop a completely integrated society or whether it will maintain and improve a partially integrated, mutually tolerant co-existence remains to be seen. The Maoris at present are a minority group and the European New Zealander is put to little effort to be tolerant. Nevertheless, racial prejudice does exist, and although small, it is a red light for the future. The present is a time of adjustment for both races, and a time which must be used effectively to encourage and further a European-style education among the Maoris so that they may take a not-inferior position in the community while at the same time retaining their Maoritanga, their own distinct culture.

After the Maori Wars and until the beginning of the twentieth century, the Maori appeared to belong to a dying race, departing from the face of New Zealand very much as the moa had done before him. The tribal structure, around which all Maori life and custom was concentrated, had been dealt a bitter blow by the Maori Land Courts and it was many years before the will to racial survival halted the falling birth rate and the slow, painful uphill journey began. That the Maori people and their leaders undertook the trek at all is a sign of uncommon courage, intelligence and flexibility.

White settlement in New Zealand is little more than 120 years old, and in that time an advanced stone-age culture has made enormous strides towards a twentieth-century technological civilisation. That there is still some distance to go is hardly surprising, but the last part of the journey might well prove to be the most difficult. It involves the whole field of Maori education, where difficulties of background as well as certain psychological reluctance to explore the mysteries of higher education must be overcome. There are some Maoris who have broken through the cultural barrier and taken university degrees, becoming doctors, lawyers, diplomats and academics, but these have been very few and are still too far between for comfort. Much more assistance is now being given to encourage Maori children to attend secondary school, but children from rural areas (where 50 per cent of the Maori population lives) would have to attend a boarding school to do so. This is a fearsome thought to a community-centred people and the pressures to leave school are very strong. Lack of home background is a big handicap; books and homework stand small chance where parents see little use for them and where study conditions are bad. This might well be said of many European homes, but the pakeha is more appreciative of the part played by education in any sort of social advancement.

The greatest handicap in the struggle for a higher educational standard lies in the problem of language. Today, nearly every Maori speaks English fluently, but speaking a language is quite different from writing or reading it and after more than half a century of basic primary education, most Maoris still do not think conceptually or abstractly in English. As many Maoris do not speak Maori at all well, this means that the majority have stopped thinking in abstract terms altogether. Principles and concepts underlie the whole structure of modern technological progress, but when confronted with so many words and ideas he cannot understand, the Maori, naturally enough, gives up. In such circumstances, vocabulary becomes very limited and the mind is not stretched beyond mundane concerns.

Most Maoris live in the northern half of the North Island and as with the pakeha there has been a substantial drift to the towns. This has caused problems of some magnitude, especially where it has revealed latent racial hostility among suburban householders who do not want Maoris for next-door neighbours, among landlords and among hotel-keepers. There has been little, if any, discrimination among employers, because the Maori is a good worker when he feels secure. His attachment to the tribal community, however, makes adjustment to city life and work very difficult, his greatest problem being that of loneliness. Maoris need the support of their community and without it they are apt to fall into anti-social habits — delinquency, leading to more serious crimes, and drunkenness, although the number of Maori alcoholics is low. Maori clubs do a great deal to help provide a community focus for the urban Maori. The incidence of Maori crime is still high, however, reflecting as it does not only the underprivileged condition of the race, but also its essentially communal attitude towards property. More Maoris are convicted for burglary, petty theft and car conversion than any other type of crime, sexual offences and crimes of violence being relatively rare among them.

At the present time, most Maoris living in cities are employed as unskilled or semi-skilled workers. As a race, they seem attracted towards power machinery — trucks, bulldozers, cranes, graders are frequently driven by Maoris who evidently enjoy their work. Unfortunately, the future is certainly going to bring a greatly increased demand for skilled workers, with a corresponding decline in the need for unskilled labourers. Education is obviously the key to the future, economically as well as socially. Maoris living in the country are nearly all employed on farms either on their own land or as labourers for someone else. Some areas of tribal land are worked as efficiently as the best pakeha farms, but this only occurs where the holdings are large enough to be properly economic and the division of tribal lands makes large holdings a rarity. Early in this century Sir Apirana Ngata assisted Maoris on the east coast to organise their land into viable units and then to raise mortgages on it to develop efficient and economic farms. Generally speaking, however, most Maori farms are still too small and their productivity is considerably lower than that of comparable pakeha farms; much Maori land is also poor land and is often remote from marketing centres. Again, limited education and training have prevented many Maori farmers from improving and modernising their farming equipment and techniques. As a result, incomes of Maori farmers are markedly lower than those of pakeha farmers. More agricultural training is an urgent need for young Maori farmers, training both in management and technique based on a broad education which includes considerable science. Otherwise, the Maori rural population will become more depressed and very conscious of the barriers separating it from the material advantages of their pakeha neighbours. The Government is undertaking large-scale development of Maori land, so that more Maori farmers can be established on their own farms. Diversification of land use is also being encouraged.

It is quite apparent that this is a critical time for the Maori race. It is also clear that the Maori people have already decided that they wish to be equal partners in the social and economic future of New Zealand, even if the next twenty years do involve an uphill grind to higher educational standards. It is not yet clear whether the reality of Maori equality will mean such a thorough integration with the European population that the race will be absorbed. Inter-marriage is common, but many of the children of such marriages officially claim their Maori, rather than their European, inheritance. This would suggest a determination to retain racial identity, and indeed, New Zealand would be the poorer without its bi-racial character. The Mormon Church has won many converts among the Maoris and has made tremendous contributions to the preservation of Maori arts as part of a living culture by establishing training centres where traditional Maori art is taught. The Maori Affairs Department has also done a great deal to foster Maoritanga, and the pakeha population is increasingly aware of what the Maori gives to the common culture. On the other hand, it would be fatally easy to preserve Maoritanga as a quaint survival from the Stone Age, becoming as irrelevant to life in modern New Zealand as Gaelic is to life in Eire.

It is significant that separate Parliamentary representation for Maoris is now being questioned, but the consensus favours the status quo in the meantime. Some Maori candidates have been nominated by both parties for European electorates; when Maoris are in fact elected to European seats the time will have arrived to review separate representation, which is widely accepted as an anachronism and very much a second best solution.

Religion in New Zealand is also at the cross-roads. The country is nominally Christian, with most of the world's major denominations represented along with numerous minor sects — some of which bear little relation to the mainstream of Christianity. Nominal adherence to the main denominations is great but actual support is much less, and impact upon the community at large is small. Over three-quarters of the population acknowledged belonging to the four main

Churches – Anglican, Presbyterian, Roman Catholic and Methodist, in that order – in answer to the (optional) question on religion at the last Census. Approximately 10 per cent took advantage of the 'object to state' alternative or denied having any religious affiliations. The remainder were widely spread among minor Protestant sects, the Eastern Orthodox Church, the Jewish religion and the indigenous religious creeds of Ratana and Ringatu – both Maori adaptations of Christianity.

Although 90 per cent of the population are nominally adherents to some creed, it is significant that only 80 per cent of marriages are performed in church. The latter percentage grossly overstates the proportion with an effective connection with religion as marriage in church rather than in a registry office is socially the done thing irrespective of the beliefs of those being married. No statistics exist of normal church attendance but a fair estimate would be a fifth, with Roman Catholics accounting for a large proportion of those going to church more or less regularly. There is no established Church but Anglican cathedrals are usually used for State occasions. There is no evidence of any marked swing away from the main denominations nor from religion as a whole but religion cannot be said to be a vital force in the country – perhaps this is a by-product of a comfortable materialist society.

It has often been jokingly observed that sport is New Zealand's main religion and, like most remarks of this nature, there is a fair measure of truth in it. There can be few countries in the world where so high a proportion of the population actively participates in sport. Rugby football is the dominant winter sport but this is of course played only by schoolboys and relatively young men. Soccer and rugby league are also played but not nearly to the same extent. These sports command massive spectator support which reaches frenzy pitch when there are inter-provincial fixtures and international matches. Then almost everyone who is not watching a game is following it on transistor radios. The power of the rugby controlling authorities is indicated by their successful resistance to the live tele-casting of matches. The rugby cult obscures the fact that many other sports are played in the winter such as hockey, golf, basketball (out-door for women, indoor for men), not to mention skiing, tramping and shooting. The mildness of New Zealand winters is very favour-able to all these activities.

In the summer cricket, tennis, bowls, fishing, yachting, baseball and softball all enjoy considerable support and swimming is very popular, but none to the same extent as rugby football. One sport of great importance remains – horse racing. This has traditionally been the closest rival to rugby as a spectator sport, perhaps because it serves as an outlet to gambling instincts as well as affording a spectacle. On-course and off-course betting is highly organised and large amounts of money change hands on a Saturday, but there are signs that the popularity of racing is declining. Strangely enough, almost all other sports are entirely free from gambling associations. Even the relatively recent innovation of national lotteries is now proving less of an attraction than when they were first introduced. Indulgence in liquor, however, shows no such decline.

Life in a small society can be dull but it has compensations; there are more opportunities for people to do things as distinct from watching other people do them. A high level of participation in sports, hobbies and community activities generally is characteristic of New Zealand. Another healthy aspect is the virtually complete absence of corruption and nepotism in public affairs. The country has produced few statesmen but even fewer rogues. Certainly wealth today plays little part in advancement to high office. Again, organised crime is not common and gangsters do not exist. It is safe for women and children to go anywhere by themselves. As the population increases, crime is likely to become more of a problem, but it is not something that concerns people today. Finally, there are of course under-privileged members of the community but slums are non-existent and racial tensions are minimal.

Chapter 10

Ambivalent Internationalism

N EW ZEALANDERS are said to be the greatest international
travellers in the world and travel statistics certainly indicate
high mobility. In 1966 almost one hundred thousand residents left the country temporarily – over 4 per cent of the population. Of course some people made more than one trip, especially to
Australia, but overseas travel is now much commoner than used to
be the case. Thus in the last decade the number going abroad has
quadrupled whereas the population has barely risen by a quarter.
This is a measure of the pull of the outside world facilitated by
cheaper air fares and increasing affluence, particularly among young
people. At one time most people travelling abroad were either
elderly folk visiting or revisiting Great Britain, variously known in
affectionate terms as 'Home' or 'Old Country', but today there are
many business travellers and young people going abroad to study or
for a working holiday. The range of countries visited is now much
wider than formerly with the United States a popular destination.

It cannot be said that understanding of other countries' problems
or appreciation of other cultures has increased proportionately with
the number of New Zealanders travelling abroad, although some
changes for the better are evident. Knowledge of Australia and the
United States in particular is more widely diffused through the
community than used to be the case. Improvements in transport and
communications do not automatically improve international understanding but they do make it harder to ignore events and conditions
elsewhere. This would seem to be how they have affected the New
Zealand man-in-the-street who is now more conscious of the outside
world but not notably more anxious to be part of it. For a country
with such a large export trade sector, there is surprisingly little sense
of community involvement in international trade. This is understandable in a sense as almost all exports are farm products and few
people now have much contact with the land. The country's heavy
reliance upon international trade has also been made less apparent

by the greater processing of imports that has occurred since the war.

Attitudes towards tourism, one of the easiest ways for New Zealand to increase its foreign exchange earnings, exemplify the common failure to associate prosperity with exporting in general as distinct from high prices for staples such as butter and wool. The prospect of greatly increased numbers of overseas visitors is not generally regarded with pleasure although their foreign currency would be very acceptable. This negative reaction is partly due to an outmoded stereotype of a tourist which survives because most tourists follow a narrow and well-defined path from port of entry to port of departure via a limited number of tourist areas. A sub-conscious but justified inferiority complex about the quality of facilities, the country's short history and its lack of cultural roots also underlies the ambivalence towards tourism. The quality and variety of scenery, of course, need no apology and other valuable tourist assets are good roads and good hygiene.

The usual overt objection to tourists is that they spoil a country for the local inhabitants but more to the point is a fear that customary values would be threatened. This is well-founded but the values in question are not particularly noble. One is the preservation of the New Zealand weekend and short shopping hours during the week. In most places shops are open from 9 a.m. to 5 p.m. Monday to Thursday, and from 9 a.m. to 9 p.m. on Fridays. By and large the only shops open at other times are dairies. This is very much a legacy of the forty-hour-week legislation passed under the first Labour Government, partly as a means of reducing unemployment. Its survival is due to the community of interest of retailers protected from effective competition and organised labour's objection to more flexible hours of work. The interests of the consumer have been substantially ignored. It is practically impossible to find a shop of any sort open on Sundays in the main urban areas. Hotels are no exception; their hours are 9 a.m. to 6 p.m. every day except Sundays. Only residents or their guests are supposed to be served outside these hours. Night clubs of any quality are virtually non-existent although good licensed restaurants are to be found in most urban areas. At the present time a referendum on liquor licensing hours is imminent, both main political parties being frightened to change the present archaic legislation without a popular mandate. The last referendum was substantially in favour of the *status quo* but this time a much narrower verdict is expected. The odds would, how-ever, appear to be against more realistic liquor laws.

Consequently New Zealand cities for the visitor are deserts at night or during the weekends. The only substantial improvement in recent years has been the licensing of high-quality restaurants where liquor may be had with meals and meal hours are more extended than usual. Some of these restaurants are very good indeed but expensive and there is a dearth of cheap reasonable eating places. In the main tourist areas shopping hours are more flexible and some entertainment is available for visitors at night. Souvenir shops of not spectacular quality are now also open at more realistic hours in the main ports of tourist entry or departure, but this innovation, like most developments associated with the tourist industry, has been agreed to reluctantly by entrepreneurs and workers alike. The distinction between a forty-hour week, which is now common in other Western countries, and shops and service establishments being open for only forty hours has yet to be fully realised. (In the case of most factory workers, of course, the working of a forty-hour week is regarded as a great hardship because of the loss of overtime.) Restricted hotel hours are bound up with the natural, but unattrac-tive, informal alliance of interests between hotel owners, who are mainly the breweries, their workers and the significant but dwindl-ing wowser[1] element in the community. The likelihood of New Zealand coming of age as regards drinking hours has already been discussed; in this as in other ways the country is adolescent.

Despite official doubts about the economic benefits of tourism and public apathy or mild antipathy, the tourist trade has expanded rapidly in the last decade. Even so, the number of overseas visitors today is no greater than in Hawaii before the tourist boom of the early 1950's. The scope for expansion in New Zealand is therefore great and international air facilities are now adequate to support a big increase. The main limitation is a shortage of high standard accommodation which in a country with high building costs is expensive. In the past a perennial problem has been the extreme seasonality of demand but this was mainly due to the overwhelming importance of New Zealand travellers. As the proportion of overseas visitors increases this will become less of a problem. Another hopeful sign is the construction of larger hotels and tourist resorts which can more easily achieve economies of scale and become profitable. A

[1] Staunch teetotaller.

major impediment to the provision of adequate accommodation for overseas visitors has been the view of major hotel operators that the 'house' could not be made to pay. It is certainly true that their houses made losses which were covered by profits from public liquor facilities but it does not follow that accommodation and restaurants cannot pay their way and earn reasonable profits given efficient management.

Personal service is regarded as menial and it is therefore difficult to staff hotels and restaurants with New Zealanders. In view of this, it is strange that more immigrants willing to work in them are not allowed into the country. The answer to this is complex but important in understanding present-day New Zealand. There are two main aspects of the immigration argument. The one concerns racial discrimination, in effect if not in principle; the other concerns the recruitment abroad of people to reduce the internal labour shortage. The former issue is less commonly debated, probably because many people feel a little guilty over the country's fairly severe limitation of Asian and southern European immigration. The principle underlying the limitation is ease of absorption and it cannot be denied that the Chinese and Indians in New Zealand keep very much to themselves and show no desire for integration. Since they have proved themselves good citizens, however, it is not immediately obvious that intergration is a necessary virtue. The practically open-door policy to Polynesian immigrants is a better justification for limiting Asian immigration. A large number of Cook Islanders, Samoans and other Pacific Islanders have settled in New Zealand in recent years and there may well be some serious absorption problems ahead. Even now the attitude of many Maoris to their Polynesian cousins is hardly cordial. This open-door policy is proper because New Zealand is a Polynesian power – if it can be called a 'power' at all – but it cannot reasonably be asked to be an Asian power as well. In practice, a little more liberality in individual cases would probably remove most of the objections to discriminatory immigration policies but one cannot help wishing that New Zealand had had more southern European immigrants since the war for the variety which they would have provided in society as well as for their labour which would be invaluable in developing the tourist industry.

The issue of large scale immigration, on the other hand, has been frequently argued. In fact every few years, when each periodic boom is at its height, employer organisations urge the Government to increase assisted immigration. Governments have so far declined to accept the argument that more immigration would cure the general labour shortage although assistance has generally been provided for workers possessing skills in particularly short supply. New Zealand is often unfavourably contrasted with Australia in this matter but the higher New Zealand rate of natural increase is usually over-looked. Since the war the populations of the two countries have in fact grown at almost the same rate. Australia's fervour for filling its empty spaces is however notably absent in New Zealand — mainly because there is much less space to fill but also because most Kiwis like an uncrowded society and the potential threat of heavily populated northern neighbours is felt much less acutely.

Employers' reasons for wanting heavier immigration are readily understandable. Two decades of more or less acute labour shortage have produced a situation of high labour mobility, absenteeism and militant unionism to which a greater influx of workers from abroad appears the obvious answer. Implicit in the employers' arguments is the thought that this would create some unemployment or at least reduce job vacancies. The standard economic answer that the state of the labour market depends more on demand than on supply has not been found convincing in employer circles but it is accepted officially. The trade union movement has generally accepted the employer association premise but of course drawn the opposite policy conclusion. Neither side appears to appreciate that to date over-full employment has been a secondary if not a primary goal of Government — at least this is the only rational conclusion to be drawn from the failure of successive administrations to take effective measures to balance supply and demand. The impossibility of financing large balance of payments deficits in future by overseas borrowing will perforce change this situation, so that pressure for more assisted immigration may be expected to disappear. In fact the situation in mid-1967 is already markedly different than at any time since the war. The conjunction of deflationary influences has produced the highest unemployment rate for a quarter century, although still low in comparison with most countries, and the probability is that it will increase still further in the next year. An immediate drop in the number of people coming to New Zealand on working holidays, notably Australians, may be expected as employment opportunities dwindle.

The underlying ground for the Government's refusal to accede to the pressure for heavier immigration in the past has been doubt about the long-term adequacy of New Zealand's raw material resources to support a large population with high living standards. This is a substantially stronger argument than the polemical answer usually given that more immigrants would increase rather than decrease inflationary pressures because of their capital requirements, especially housing. Unlike Australia, New Zealand's mineral base is weak and no conceivable immigration intake could provide a domestic market large enough to realise economies of scale over a wide range of products. This realisation greatly strengthens the case for international specialisation and trade, New Zealand's historical road to affluence, in spite of the many barriers to easy movement of goods between nations today.

The fear of the Labour movement that heavier immigration would depress workers' standards of living reflects the same attitude of mind that opposes imports from countries with low labour costs. The 'sweated labour' argument is less commonly heard now than formerly and this may owe something to New Zealanders' increasing appreciation of the problems of developing countries. Government cannot be said to have led public opinion on this issue, rather the reverse. Indeed, official efforts to ensure that no New Zealand manufacturer suffered as a result of the Limited Free Trade Agreement with Australia were almost ludicrously paternal. At the same time it must be admitted that the Australian Government also displays a singular lack of faith in the mutual advantage of the Agreement to the two countries.

A similar hesitancy is evident in New Zealand's trading relations with other countries, especially Japan. In part this reflects an understandable unwillingness to erode the considerable preferences enjoyed by British goods on the New Zealand market at a time when it is obviously important to retain some bargaining strength. The renewed prospect of the United Kingdom joining the European Economic Community is, however, prompting a closer scrutiny of the British undertaking to look after New Zealand's 'special interest' in this event. The uncomfortable feeling of having to stand on one's own feet is growing and this largely explains the country's ambivalence to the world at large. The issue of internationalism versus insularity has yet to be resolved in people's minds although there is no choice; the country is too small to go it alone and the cost of attempting to do so would be prohibitive. The disappointing consequences for New Zealand of the Kennedy Round has given strength to the arguments of those favouring bilateral trade but very few promising two-way trade possibilities suggest themselves. New Zealand's main customers for many years to come are likely to be the industrialised countries of the Northern Hemisphere but these are also strongly protectionist so far as agricultural products are concerned. Japan is the only ray of sunshine but to clear the fog properly New Zealand will probably have to cut many of its ties with Great Britain and possibly Australia also.

Ever since the fall of Singapore in 1942, New Zealand has looked to the United States for leadership in the Pacific. There is little doubt that most Kiwis are well disposed towards Americans but events in Vietnam have somewhat strained this rapport. The number of pacifists in New Zealand is negligible and the extravagant propaganda of the small but vocal group of militant Vietnam peacemongers has done more to make the country's support of the United States in Vietnam acceptable than rational argument by Government. The attitude of the majority of people is that the United States has no alternative today but to see the conflict to a conclusion, however ill-advised its involvement in the first place. Whatever importance Government attaches to the SEATO Pact with its obligation for New Zealand to support the South Vietnamese, the public feeling is that the country intervened in order to demonstrate solidarity with the United States and Australia because of community of interest with these powers.

Increased American interest in New Zealand businesses is, however, viewed with some trepidation. More generally, the country's ambivalent internationalism is well shown up in attitudes towards overseas investment, from whatever source. It is widely accepted that often the only way to share in technological progress is to accept capital from abroad and no one objects to the assistance this affords the balance of payments; but the fear of being taken over and exploited is present nevertheless. So far anyway, few New Zealand enterprises have shown much interest in extending their operations overseas. This probably reflects their unsureness of themselves. In sharp contrast are the widespread equity holdings of individual New Zealanders in other countries, especially Australia. A sound instinct may be evident here for New Zealand businesses are not notably well managed, labour relations are often difficult and the scale of operations is generally too small to permit maximum profitability. The partial alternative to overseas investment of reducing consumption and increasing savings has evidently little attraction for anyone.

In the past thirty years overseas investment has been intimately associated with import licensing as foreign suppliers have endeavoured to preserve their markets in New Zealand, if not by bringing in goods made abroad, at least by local manufacture. That the latter has been frequently uneconomic is disguised by import licensing to the point that devaluation may prove the only way to achieve freedom of trade without causing serious unemployment. Naturally three decades of restrictions on imports have created significant pressure groups in favour of their continuance, viz. manufacturers enjoying massive but concealed protection, their employees and importers who would suffer if goods could be freely imported from any source. The disadvantages of import licensing are, however, now becoming very apparent and New Zealand's final turning away from insularity may well be signalled by the removal of quantitative restrictions on importing as soon as the present balance of payments problems have been overcome.

Outward-looking forces are now more clearly in the ascendant than for some time. The country is changing over to decimal currency in 1967 and significantly has adopted the dollar rather than the pound as the new currency unit. Tourism is expanding rapidly although without much purposeful official encouragement. Overseas diplomatic and trade representation is being increased. The country now belongs to the International Monetary Fund and the World Bank, despite vigorous opposition at the time the decision to join was made in 1961. In this case the desire for further overseas borrowing facilities was probably the main factor influencing Government but it was accepted that joining represented some additional involvement in the world. New Zealand troops are serving in Vietnam and Malaysia and police in Cyprus. There is a growing interest in Asian languages and Asian affairs generally. Finally, closer cooperation with Australia is now being attempted despite sometimes justifiable misgivings about the bona fides of the Australians.

Popular support for aid to developing countries has also increased, or at least become more articulate, in recent years. Government aid is still very small in relation to Gross National Product (about one-tenth of one per cent) but private aid compares favourably with other developed countries. Renewed pressure on Government to increase its foreign aid programme may be expected in the near future. The striking growth of the New Zealand volunteer movement, despite limited Government support, is an indication of the groundswell of opinion.

All of these developments point to a greater awareness of international interdependence. Obvious relics of a more insular attitude still exist such as import licensing, stringent foreign exchange control, visa requirements where none are necessary and a peculiar blindness towards New Zealand's opportunities and responsibilities in the South Pacific. This was the area of New Zealand's early imperialist dreams; their non-fulfilment seems to have been traumatic, for politically and commercially the Pacific has been largely neglected ever since. Where New Zealand has intervened, as in Western Samoa and the Cook Islands, its efforts have generally been half-hearted. At present there is a great danger that interest in South-east Asia will divert attention from the Pacific. This would be unfortunate because New Zealand's efforts in the East cannot be more than a drop in the bucket whereas the resources required to set the South Pacific Islands on the road to sound economic and social development are within New Zealand's capacity to supply. The trade advantages of channelling foreign aid to the South Pacific may not in the long run be great but the psychological benefit to New Zealand would be substantial. Success in helping its small immediate neighbours to achieve viable economies would give New Zealand the confidence it needs to face the outside world on its own account.

A Short Outline of the Constitutional
History of New Zealand

I N 1770 Captain James Cook took possession of the islands of
New Zealand in the name of King George III, but nothing was
done to substantiate the claim until 1833 when, reluctantly, the
British Government appointed James Busby as British Resident, to
look after the interests of British subjects in a particularly lawless
part of the world. It quickly became apparent, however, that
Britain would have to undertake complete responsibility for the
territory. By the signing of the 'Treaty' of Waitangi in 1840 New
Zealand became a British colony by occupation if not by treaty.

For a few months New Zealand was placed under the jurisdiction
of the Colony of New South Wales, until arrangements could be
made for its legal existence as a separate colony. This was done in
the 'Charter for Erecting the Colony of New Zealand', naming the
three main islands New Ulster, New Munster and New Leinster, and
providing a structure of Government: Governor plus Executive
Council comprising Colonial Secretary, Attorney-General and
Colonial Treasurer. There was also provision for a Legislative
Council of seven members: Governor, members of the Executive
Council and three nominated Justices of Peace.

In practice, however, Governor Hobson and his successors administered the Colony without help, calling together the Executive
and Legislative Councils only infrequently. Naturally enough, the
growing number of settlers became restive for a form of representative government. The Wellington (New Zealand Company) settlers
had considerable influence in London and in 1846 an absurdly
complex constitution was framed, providing indeed settler representation but under a system of administration which was bound to
collapse under its own weight. Governor Grey was able to provide
several reasonable arguments to delay the practical operation of the
Constitution; it may have been that he was too fond of his auto-
cratic position to let such power pass easily from his hands, but

certainly the 1846 Constitution would have delivered the Maoris and
their lands into the hands of the settlers. He convinced the British
Government that the Colony was not yet ready for self-government,
although he did take the preliminary step of dividing New Zealand
into the two provinces of New Ulster and New Munster.

After constant and indignant pressure from the settlers, Grey sent
a draft constitution to London, and the Colonial Office framed a
new constitution which owed much to these suggestions. The New
Zealand Constitution Act was passed in 1852 and remains the basis
of the modern constitutional structure of New Zealand. The dia-
grammatic representation gives a clear picture:

Governor (appointed by Crown)
General Assembly = Legislative Council (appointed)
House of Representatives (elected for five years)

Six provincial governments were also established, each composed of
a Provincial Council of nine members presided over by a Super-
intendent.

The modifications of this framework make up New Zealand's
constitutional history; most of the alterations were commonsense,
and were achieved with little fuss. The 1852 Act provided for a
wide franchise which was completely without racial bias, although
in fact the property qualification effectively excluded the Maoris
with their system of tribal land holding. In practice the House of
Representatives immediately adopted the system of responsible
government by Cabinet; the Governor was bound to act on the
advice of Ministers with a majority in the House of Representatives except in the case of Maori affairs or external affairs. There
were, however, provisions in the Act which made New Zealand still
conscious of its colonial status:

1. The New Zealand Parliament could not pass laws repugnant to
   the legislation of Great Britain.
2. Great Britain could pass legislation applying to New Zealand
   and could override New Zealand legislation.
3. There was no provision in the Act for extra-territorial legislation.
4. The Governor was given the power to reserve New Zealand
   legislation for the assent of the Crown.
5. The Crown could disallow legislation even when the Governor
   had passed it.

A number of amendments to the Act were made as they became necessary, but New Zealand showed itself remarkably slow to sever its ties with Britain, preferring a token legal subservience to a show of independence which might be considered either premature or harmful, although in 1871 and again in 1887 it pressed unsuccessfully for the right to negotiate its own trade agreements.

In 1867 (after the Maori Wars) four separate Maori seats were established in Parliament, the members to be elected by manhood suffrage. The year 1876 saw the abolition of the provincial governments amid bitter political in-fighting. It was very apparent, however, that the progress of the country was being seriously retarded by the jealous bickering of the provincial governments, haggling over land development and its finance.

In 1879 manhood suffrage without a property qualification was established. The House of Representatives was also elected for three years, instead of the original five of the Act. Women were enfranchised in 1893.

New Zealand became a Dominion in 1907 although little seems to have been meant by the title. Probably it drew attention to the very pro-British sentiment of New Zealand at that time. Much more important were the Imperial Conferences of 1923, 1926 and 1931, where the constitutional problems of Commonwealth countries were discussed and legal anomalies were brought out into the open. At the 1923 and 1926 Conferences it was agreed that Dominions could make their own trading arrangements – a decision of which New Zealand took almost immediate advantage. The role of the Governor was also discussed; his was an ambiguous position, being at once the representative of the Crown (as a constitutional monarch) and the official envoy to New Zealand of the interests of the British Parliament. New Zealand was slow to adopt the solution provided by the Imperial Conferences, but in 1939 a High Commissioner was appointed to represent the United Kingdom's interest in New Zealand, leaving the Governor-General free to fulfil much the same role as the King in Britain.

In 1931 the British Parliament enacted the Statute of Westminster, legislation which gave complete constitutional sovereignty to British Dominions, while at the same time asserting the ties of Commonwealth. Canada and South Africa adopted the Statute immediately, but New Zealand (and Australia) did not see the need for a further statement of their constitutional position. During the

Second World War, however, New Zealand asserted its right to complete independence, differing from Britain over several important issues. These differences of opinion, however friendly, were certainly instrumental in New Zealand's final adoption of the Statute of Westminster in 1947.

New Zealand's early Prime Ministers soon realised the need, if not for an independent foreign policy, at least for consultation with the British Government before the country was committed to wars on behalf of the United Kingdom. During the First World War the Imperial War Cabinet went some way towards meeting the need, and the discussions of the 1917 Imperial War Conference allowed the right of the Dominions to a voice in shaping foreign policy. Techniques of consultation were set up between the wars, but it became apparent by the time of the Second World War that the Dominions would require complete autonomy in their external affairs, and this is the position today.

In 1950 the House of Representatives abolished the Legislative Council. The Liberal Government in 1891 had found the conservative Council a barrier to its policies; it had forced the Governor to accept its appointees to the Council, at the same time limiting the term of appointment to seven years only. From this time onwards the Council's influence waned, until by the time of its abolition it had ceased to play any significant role in the government of the country.

New Zealand stepped outside the tradition of British legislation in 1962 to appoint an Ombudsman, a Parliamentary Commissioner for Investigations responsible directly to Parliament. Following Scandinavian custom, the Ombudsman is required to be accessible to any person who has a grievance against officialdom; the Ombudsman investigates all cases which come before him and where appropriate presents a report with recommendations to Parliament. In a bureaucracy like New Zealand such an office has probably an important part to play in the day to day work of democracy.

Today, New Zealand is in all respects a completely independent nation; the Queen is the Queen of New Zealand whose representative in New Zealand is the Governor-General. New Zealand is a free and independent member of the Commonwealth, claiming equality with the other members of that group of nations, acknowledging by virtue of historical accident and ties of blood a 'mutual confidence and co-operation' in 'an association from which every element of constraint has vanished'.

Export Receipts, Import Payments and Net Invisible Payments Overseas, and Balance of Payments, 1950/1–1967/8 (£ million)

March Year	Export Receipts (f.o.b.)	Overseas Payments etc.*	Surplus (+) or Deficit (−)
1950/1	203	176	+27
1951/2	251	282	−31
1952/3	239	244	− 5
1953/4	246	211	+35
1954/5	236	273	−37
1955/6	263	291	−28
1956/7	274	287	−13
1957/8	270	314	−44
1958/9	264	283	−19
1959/60	312	270	+42
1960/1	287	340	−53
1961/2	290	345	−55
1962/3	303	326	−23
1963/4	359	376	−17
1964/5	379	404	−25
1965/6	375	468	−93
1966/7	370	480	−110
1967/8	395	465	−70

* Import payments f.o.b. plus the difference between overseas payments and receipts, other than for imports and exports, which in New Zealand's case is always positive.

Source: For the period 1950/1–1965/6, Official Balance of Payments estimates; for the last two years shown, N.Z. Institute of Economic Research.

Appendix 3

Consumer, Public Authority and Private Capital Spending, 1950/1–1967/8 (£ million)

March Year	Personal Consumption	Public Authority	Private Capital
1950/1	416	127	76
1951/2	472	146	93
1952/3	471	180	101
1953/4	524	192	108
1954/5	602	195	138
1955/6	640	218	133
1956/7	665	239	128
1957/8	724	251	144
1958/9	731	258	145
1959/60	738	275	149
1960/1	862	289	183
1961/2	900	303	196
1962/3	944	325	196
1963/4	1005	351	215
1964/5	1084	386	249
1965/6	1195	422	277
1966/7	1295	460	280
1967/8	1380	485	270

Source: For the period 1950/1–1965/6 Official National Income estimates; for the last two years shown, N.Z. Institute of Economic Research.

Bibliography

Social Science, Social Welfare, and Statistics

Brown, B. M.: *The Rise of New Zealand Labour; a History of the New Zealand Labour Party from 1916 to 1940*, Wellington, Price Milburn, 1962.

Gordon, B. K.: *New Zealand Becomes a Pacific Power*, Chicago, University of Chicago Press, 1960.

Larkin, T. C., ed.: *New Zealand's External Relations*, Wellington, N.Z. Institute of Public Administration; London, O.U.P., 1962.

Scott, K. J., ed.: *Welfare in New Zealand*, Wellington, N.Z. Institute of Public Administration; London, O.U.P., 1955.

Economics and Banking

Blyth, C. A., ed.: *The Future of Manufacturing in New Zealand*, Wellington, N.Z. Institute of Public Administration; London, O.U.P., 1964.

Reserve Bank of New Zealand: *Money and Banking in New Zealand*, Wellington, 1963.

— *Overseas Trade and Finance, with Particular Reference to New Zealand*, Wellington, 1960.

Simkin, C. G. F.: *The Instability of a Dependent Economy: Economic Fluctuations in New Zealand, 1840–1914*, London, O.U.P., 1951.

Government and Public Administration

Polaschek, R. J.: *Government Administration in New Zealand*, Wellington, N.Z. Institute of Public Administration; London, O.U.P., 1958.

Education

Ashton-Warner, S.: *Teacher*, New York, Simon & Schuster; London, Secker & Warburg, 1963.

The Maori People, Past and Present

Barrow, T. T.: *The Decorative Arts of the New Zealand Maori*, Wellington, Reed, 1964.

179

Best, E.: *The Maori As He Was*, Wellington, Govt. Print., 1952.

Buck, Sir P.: *The Coming of the Maori*, Wellington, Whitcombe & Tombs, 1949.

Firth, R. W.: *Economics of the New Zealand Maori*, 2nd ed., Wellington, Govt. Print., 1959.

Grey, Sir G.: *Polynesian Mythology and Ancient Traditional History of the Maori*, Christchurch, Whitcombe & Tombs, 1956.

Ritchie, J. E.: *The Making of a Maori; a Case Study of a Changing Community*, Wellington, Reed, 1963.

Geology and Earth Science

Cotton, Sir C. A.: *Geomorphology*, 7th rev. ed., Christchurch, Whitcombe & Tombs, 1958.

Salmon, J. H. M.: *A History of Goldmining in New Zealand*, Wellington, Govt. Print., 1963.

Williams, G. J.: *Economic Geology of New Zealand*, Melbourne, Australasian Institute of Mining and Metallurgy, 1965.

Flora

Allan, H. H.: *Flora of New Zealand*, Wellington, Govt. Print., 1961 – 3 vols. Vol. 1, 1961.

Cockayne, L.: *The Vegetation of New Zealand*, 3rd ed. (Reprint), Weinheim, H. R. Engelmann (J. Cramer), 1958.

Guthrie-Smith, W. H.: *Tutira; the Story of a New Zealand Sheep Station*, 3rd ed., Edinburgh, William Blackwood, 1953.

Wall, A., and Allan, H. H.: *The Botanical Names of the Flora of New Zealand; their Origin, History and Meaning*, 2nd ed., Christchurch, Whitcombe & Tombs, 1950.

Agriculture, Forestry, etc.

Duff, O. A.: *Shepherd's Calendar*, Hamilton, Paul's Book Arcade, 1961 (i.e. 1962).

Studholme, E. C.: *Te Waimate: Early Station Life in New Zealand*, 2nd ed., Wellington, Reed, 1954.

Language, Maori and English

Wall, A.: *The Mother Tongue in New Zealand*, Wellington, Reed, 1936.

Sport

Pascoe, J. D.: *Great Days in New Zealand Mountaineering*, Wellington, Reed, 1958.

Swan, A. C.: *History of New Zealand Rugby Football*, Vol. 2: *1946–57*, Wellington, N.Z. Rugby Football Union, 1958.

— *History of New Zealand Rugby Football 1870–1945*, Wellington, N.Z. Rugby Football Union by Reed, 1948.

Literature, General

McCormick, E. H.: *New Zealand Literature; a Survey*, London, O.U.P., 1959.

Stevens, J.: *The New Zealand Novel, 1860–1960*, Wellington, Reed, 1963.

Poetry

Chapman, R. McD., and Bennett, J., comps.: *Anthology of New Zealand Verse*, London, O.U.P., 1956.

Curnow, T. A. M.: *The Penguin Book of New Zealand Verse*, Harmondsworth, Eng., Penguin Books, 1960.

Fiction

Ashton-Warner, S.: *Spinster*, London, Secker & Warburg, 1958.

Courage, J.: *The Young Have Secrets*, London, Cape, 1954.

Cross, I. R.: *The God Boy*, London, A. Deutsch, 1958.

Duggan, M. N.: *Summer in the Gravel Pit*, Stories, Hamilton, Blackwood & Janet Paul; London, Gollancz, 1965.

Frame, J.: *Owls Do Cry*, Christchurch, Pegasus Press, 1957.

Lee, J. A.: *Shining With the Shiner*, London, May Fair Books, 1963.

Mansfield, K.: *Selected Stories*, chosen and introduced by D. M. Davin, London, O.U.P., 1953.

Mulgan, J. A. E.: *Man Alone*, Hamilton, Paul's Book Arcade, 1960.

Sargeson, F.: *Collected Stories*, Hamilton, Blackwood & Janet Paul, 1964.

Satchell, W.: *The Greenstone Door*, London, Whitcombe & Tombs, 1950.

Shadbolt, M.: *The New Zealanders*, London, Gollancz, 1959.

Fiction, Juvenile

Duggan, M. N.: *Falter Tom and the Water Boy*, Hamilton, Paul's Book Arcade, 1958.

Morice, S.: *The Book of Wiremu*, Hamilton, Paul's Book Arcade, 1958.

Westra, A.: *Washday at the Pa*, Christchurch, Caxton Press, 1964.

Essays

Holcroft, M. H.: *Discovered Isles; a Trilogy: The Deepening Stream, The Waiting Hills, Encircling Seas*, Christchurch, Caxton Press, 1950.

Plays

Jones, S.: *The Tree*, Christchurch, Whitcombe & Tombs, 1960.

Humour

Reid, J. C.: *The Kiwi Laughs; an Anthology of New Zealand Prose Humour*, Wellington, Reed, 1960.

Descriptive Works — General

Ausubel, D. P.: *The Fern and the Tiki; an American View of New Zealand*, Sydney, Angus & Robertson, 1960.

Bigwood, K. V.: *New Zealand in Colour*, Wellington, Reed, 1961–1962, 2 vols.

McLintock, A. H., ed.: *A Descriptive Atlas of New Zealand*, Wellington, Govt. Print., 1959.

Wood, F. L. W.: *This New Zealand*, 3rd ed., Hamilton, Paul's Book Arcade, 1958.

Descriptive Works — Historical

Barker, M. A. (Lady): *Station Life in New Zealand*, Christchurch, Whitcombe & Tombs, 1950.

Butler, S.: *A First Year in Canterbury Settlement*, edited by A. C. Brassington and P. B. Maling, Hamilton, Blackwood & Janet Paul, 1964.

Cook, J.: *The Journals of Captain James Cook on his Voyages of Discovery*, edited by J. C. Beaglehole, Cambridge, Hakluyt Society, 1955.

Drummond, Mrs. A. E. H.: *Married and Gone to New Zealand; Being Extracts from the Writings of Women Pioneers*, London, O.U.P.; Hamilton, Paul's Book Arcade, 1960.

Maning, F. E.: *Old New Zealand; a Tale of the Good Old Times*, Christchurch, Whitcombe & Tombs, 1952.

Pascoe, J. D.: *The Mountains, the Bush and the Sea; a Photographic Report*, Christchurch, Whitcombe & Tombs, 1950.

Historical Works — General and Period Including Maori Wars

Beaglehole, J. C.: *The Discovery of New Zealand*, 2nd ed., London, O.U.P., 1961.

Condliffe, J. B.: *New Zealand in the Making*, 2nd ed., London, Allen & Unwin, 1959.

— *The Welfare State in New Zealand*, London, Allen & Unwin, 1959.

Gorst, Sir J. E.: *The Maori King*, edited by Keith Sinclair, London, O.U.P.; Hamilton, Paul's Book Arcade, 1959.

McLintock, A. H.: *Crown Colony Government in New Zealand*, Wellington, Govt. Print., 1958.

Miller, J. O.: *Early Victorian New Zealand 1839–52*, London, O.U.P., 1958.

Morrell, W. P.: *The Great Powers in the Pacific*, London, published for the Historical Association by Routledge and Kegan Paul, 1963.

Oliver, W. H.: *The Story of New Zealand*, 2nd ed., London, Faber, 1963.

Ross, A.: *New Zealand Aspirations in the Pacific in the Nineteenth Century*, Oxford, Clarendon Press, 1964.

Sinclair, K.: *A History of New Zealand*, Penguin Books, 1959.

— *The Origins of the Maori Wars*, Wellington, New Zealand University Press, 1957.

Sutch, W. B.: *The Quest for Security in New Zealand*, Penguin Books, 1942.

World War, 1914–18

Official History of New Zealand's Effort in the Great War, Auckland, Whitcombe & Tombs, under authority of N.Z. Govt., 4 vols., 1919–23.

World War, 1939–45

Baker, J. V. T.: *The New Zealand People at War; War Economy*, Wellington, War History Branch, 1965.

Wood, F. L. W.: *The New Zealand People at War; Political and External Affairs*, Wellington, War History Branch, 1958.

Biography

Alpers, A. F. G.: *Katherine Mansfield; a Biography*, New York, Knopf; London, Cape, 1954.

Lee, J. A.: *Simple on a Soap-box*, Auckland, Collins, 1963.

Sinclair, K.: *William Pember Reeves; New Zealand Fabian*, Oxford, Clarendon Press, 1965.

Index

Music, 135, 136, 137
Musical and dramatic societies, 136

Nairn, James McLachlan, 139
Napier, 24, 25
Nash, Sir Walter, 71, 74, 75, 82, 84
National Airways Corporation, 111
National Health Service, 74, 79
National Mortgage Corporation, 70, 73
National Orchestra, 135, 136, 137
National Party, 74, 75, 79, 81, 82, 83, 84, 86, 88, 110, 111, 117, 119
Nationalisation, 60, 70, 74, 79, 82
Nationalism, 48
National Youth Orchestra, 136
Natural gas, 24, 101; Kapuni, 106
Nelson, 25, 43, 45, 46, 47, 102, 147
New Leinster, 173
New Munster, 173, 174
New Plymouth, 23, 24, 43, 45, 46, 47, 48, 100, 101
New South Wales, colony of, 173
New Ulster, 174
New Zealand Alliance for the Suppression and Prohibition of the Liquor Traffic, 151, 152
New Zealand Company, 43, 44, 147, 150, 173
New Zealand Forest Service, 99
New Zealand Institute of Economic Research, 177, 178
New Zealand Players, 134
News Media Bill, 88
Newspapers, 133
Ngata, Sir Apirana, 66, 160
Ninety Mile Beach, 36
Nordmeyer, Arnold, 84
North Island, 17, 19, 20, 22, 24, 26, 27, 28, 29, 30, 38, 39, 40, 43, 44, 46, 47, 49, 50, 51, 52, 95, 101, 102, 106, 134, 159
Northern Hemisphere, 170
Northland, 19, 22, 30
Novelists, 128, 130
Nuie, 21

Oil, 22, 100, 101, 103
Oliver, W. H., 130
Ombudsman, 176
Opera, 136
Opera Company, 136
Opposition, 63, 75, 80, 84, 117

Orthodox Church, 162
Otago and Southland, 19, 24, 27, 28, 29, 35, 40, 45, 53, 101, 102, 146, 150, 152
Overseas capital, 56, 57, 74, 170, 171
Overseas reserves, 74, 76, 83, 87, 114, 119
Overtime, 73, 123, 166
Oysters, 27

Pacific, 15, 21, 75, 76, 77, 78, 81, 89, 133, 172
Pakistan, 89
Palaeozoic period, 29
Palmerston North, 25
Parliament, structure of, 110
Parochialism, 16, 17, 46, 138, 153
Pearl Harbor, 77
Philippines, 89
Philistinism, 128
Picton, 25, 26
Plant ecology, 30, 31
Pleistocene period, 29
Poetry, 127, 129, 132
Police Offences Bill, 82, 83
Polling system, 110
Polynesian, 23, 38, 39, 66, 89, 167
Pomare, Sir Maui, 66
Pompallier, Bishop John Baptist Francis, 41
Population, 15, 17, 19, 20, 22, 23, 24, 25, 27, 106, 160, 164
Port Chalmers, 59
Post Office, 105, 106, 107, 108, 111
Pottery, 137
Poverty Bay—Hawkes Bay, 24, 25
Pragmatism, 17, 18, 52, 81, 85, 124, 130, 133, 149
Presbyterians, 45, 146, 162
Pressure groups, 18, 120, 151, 171
Price Tribunal, 76
Prices: export, 67, 87, 96, 113, 121; guaranteed, 123; internal, 78, 79, 81, 120; land, 63, 68; overseas, 55, 62, 68, 70, 74, 76, 101, 117; wheat, 57; wool, 56, 57, 83, 96, 117, 120, 121
Primary industry, 20, 92, 93, 94, 95
Primary Produce Processing, 102
Private enterprise, 68, 79, 86, 111, 122
Privy Council, 56

Printed in Great Britain by
Western Printing Services Limited
Bristol